DAUGHTER
OF PRUSSIA

Princess Louise of Prussia

DAUGHTER
OF PRUSSIA

LOUISE, GRAND DUCHESS
OF BADEN AND HER FAMILY

JOHN VAN DER KISTE

A & F

First published 2017

A & F Publications,
South Brent, Devon, England TQ10 9AS

ISBN-13: 978-1546960379
ISBN-10: 1546960376

Typeset 11pt Georgia

Printed by CreateSpace

CONTENTS

Illustrations   2

Introduction   5

Daughter of the Emperor   7

Aunt of the Emperor   63

Genealogical tables   105

Chronology   109

Reference notes   113

Bibliography   117

Index   121

ILLUSTRATIONS

Princess Louise of Prussia   *frontispiece*

Map: Germany in the nineteenth century   *page 15*

Between pages 46 and 63

William I, German Emperor
Augusta, German Empress
King Frederick William IV of Prussia
Princess Louise of Prussia, 1856
Louise and Frederick, Grand Duke and Duchess of
  Baden, at the time of their engagement, 1856
Prince and Princess Frederick William of Prussia,
  c.1860
Louise, Grand Duchess of Baden, in the early years of
  her marriage
The Grand Duke and Duchess of Baden with the
  Crown Prince and Princess of Prussia, in mourning
  for King Frederick William IV, 1861
Frederick, Grand Duke of Baden, c.1865
The Grand Duchess of Baden and her daughter
  Victoria, c.1866
The Grand Duchess of Baden and her son Louis,
  c.1870
The Grand Duchess of Baden and her children, c.1871

Clara Barton, who assisted the Grand Duchess in nursing work during the Franco-Prussian war

The proclamation of the German Empire at Versailles, January 1871, with Emperor William I, Crown Prince Frederick William, Grand Duke Frederick of Baden, and Prince Otto von Bismarck

Alice, Grand Duchess of Hesse and the Rhine, c.1875

Crown Prince Frederick William of Prussia, c.1880

Between pages 92 and 105

Princess Victoria of Baden and Crown Prince Gustav of Sweden, 1881

Crown Princess Victoria of Sweden and her sons

Prince and Princess William of Prussia and their eldest son William, 1887

The Empress Frederick, c.1896

Queen Victoria of Sweden with Prince Max von Baden and King Gustav V (right), c.1910

Louise and Frederick, Grand Duke and Duchess of Baden, c.1906

The Grand Duke and Duchess of Baden, 1906

Mainau Castle

Louise, Grand Duchess of Baden, c.1910

Louise, Grand Duchess of Baden, c.1914

Louise, Grand Duchess of Baden, in her last years

Frederick II, the last Grand Duke of Baden

Queen Victoria of Sweden in her last years

INTRODUCTION

P RINCESS Louise Marie Elizabeth of Prussia, later Grand Duchess of Baden, is a somewhat shadowy figure in the annals of the house of Hohenzollern. One of two children of Prince William (later King of Prussia and subsequently first German Emperor) and his consort Princess Augusta, and only sibling of the future Emperor Frederick, she had little impact on the age in which she lived. Like most of her contemporaries, she undertook much charitable and nursing work. In the words of her nephew, later Emperor William II, she was 'a model sovereign princess'. (A less charitable observer might have construed that verdict as 'she knew her place'). She made no effort to involve herself with issues of the day, except from a brief attempt to intercede with her father on behalf of Catholics at the time of the *Kulturkampf.*

Otherwise, for the most part she and her husband Frederick, the Grand Duke, lived relatively quiet lives. Her eighty-four years began during the era when Prussia was just one German state of several, and ended after the First World War, just as the Weimar republic was about to come into existence. Twelve years older than his wife, the Grand Duke lived to be eighty-one, and was spared the outbreak of the war which he had dreaded and perhaps foreseen.

Both played a supportive role towards the German Emperors, although Louise like others in her family occasionally incurred the suspicion of Chancellor Bismarck, as did so many of her contemporaries. Above all, it is from their daughter that the last two monarchs – as well as the future one – of Sweden are descended.

This book had its origins in an article I originally wrote and published in *Royalty Digest*, 'Louise, Grand Duchess of Baden: A model sovereign princess' (No. 121, July 2001), and I am pleased to have this opportunity of expanding it into book form.

John Van der Kiste

1. DAUGHTER OF THE EMPEROR

I

O N 11 June 1829 the thirty-two-year-old Prince William of Prussia, second son of King Frederick William III, married Princess Augusta of Saxe-Weimar Eisenach. A true Hohenzollern, William was a dedicated soldier with no interest in the arts or anything else outside military affairs, and it was no secret that he had been passionately in love with Elise Radziwill, a member of the Polish nobility who were not considered sufficiently high-born to marry members of the Hohenzollern dynasty of Prussia. Augusta was a lively seventeen-year-old who had been brought up in the state of Weimar to appreciate the fine arts, particularly painting, drawing and music, and to take a keen interest in the questions of the day. To those who knew them well it was evident that both were merely doing what was expected of them, and that it was anything but a love match.

Two years later, on 18 October 1831, she gave birth to a son and heir, Prince Frederick William, always known in the family as 'Fritz'. With the new dignity of motherhood, she now displayed a new sense of pride and aloofness. Whereas she had formerly been a little hesitant, nervous, even uncertain of her ground in Prussia, now she could feel that she meant something to the family into which she had married, especially as the Crown Prince and Princess were still childless and that situation seemed unlikely to change. Now that she had she had provided an heir to the throne in the younger generation, she was more respected by the rest of a family who were not over-friendly towards her. However, within a short time of marriage she had developed such an aversion to her husband that they did not have another child for seven years. She was however said to have had at least one or two miscarriages.

Princess Louise Marie Elizabeth of Prussia was born on 3 December 1838. The first of these names had been chosen in memory of Prince William's mother Queen Louise, who died comparatively young. Husband and wife were evidently making the best of an unsatisfactory marriage, and there would be no more children. With the arrival of this daughter, Augusta declared that her duties towards the perpetuation of the ruling dynasty were now complete.

Eighteen months later, on 7 June 1840, King Frederick William III died, and his childless eldest son ascended the throne as King Frederick William IV. William, who was his junior by little more than a year, became heir to the throne. On the day after the funeral of their father, he was given the title Prince of Prussia, created Governor of Pomerania, and made Commander in Chief of the Prussian infantry, a responsibility he took on with some pride.

While Frederick William IV had been heir to the throne, he had been seen by the Prussians as having the makings of a modern-minded King, sufficiently aware of the mood of changing times to grant them a constitution. He marked his accession, as monarchs so often did in those days, by granting a pardon to all political offenders. At the same time he demonstrated an awareness of the sense of regal pageantry demanded by his subjects. Life at court now became more conspicuous, more picturesque, as he began to surround himself with a state and magnificence unheard of or unseen by those who recalled the parsimony of his father. For the first time, even artists and poets were invited to the capital. All this demonstrated a step in the right direction, which enlightened spirits such as Princess Augusta found more than welcome.

However, those who expected they would see Prince William and his consort occupy a more important position at court before long had calculated without reference to the new Queen. Born a princess of Bavaria, Elizabeth had always barely tolerated her sister-in-law, now Princess of Prussia, and she never lost an opportunity of treating her with scorn in public. Louise also grew up to fear this formidable and unfriendly woman.

One day the infant Princess Louise was brought back to the palace after a drive, when the attention of her nurse in charge temporarily wandered. Instead of making sure that the child was safe in front of her, she let her follow her into the room. The little girl immediately ran towards the open window, which fortunately for her was on the first floor, and fell out. Nobody was sure whether she fell into the arms of a passing apprentice, or into those of the sentry on watch, walking backwards and forwards in front of the Castle. In in the event somebody managed to catch her, and she was none the worse for her accident. The nurse was not dismissed, and neither father nor mother even reproached her for her carelessness, for, they argued, 'as God has preserved our child, we have no right to punish a human being for the misfortune which might have befallen her.'[1]

William never showed more than perfunctory affection for his son, but he always doted on his daughter. When Louise was a child, he only had to appear unannounced in the schoolroom for her to put her work aside so she could climb on to his knee. Despite the teacher's half-hearted protests, in no time they would be playing together on the floor. This never happened when the more remote Augusta came in, for then, it was noticed, the little girl suddenly seemed to become rather intimidated.

> Louise involuntarily drew herself up to her dull height, and sat stiff and constrained as for her portrait, while she inwardly trembled lest her answers should prove incorrect .... her mother's presence filled her with awe.[2]

With her artistic interests, Augusta was keen to see that her daughter received a good education. Nevertheless she was very narrow-minded, and had ordered the tutors that they were to remove anything that smacked of questionable morals from her history books. Louise therefore believed that King Louis XIV of France had had three wives, and one day she innocently asked why the Pope had allowed it.[3]

As there was a gap in age of seven years between them, while she was very small Louise and her brother were never particularly close. However, this had lessened by the time of his early maturity. When she was about twelve or thirteen, they sometimes visited their mother's rural retreat in Coblenz, West Prussia, and the two of them were to be seen in each others' company. They enjoyed strolling along the banks of the river Elbe, shopping in the nearby towns, or going to explore the fairs, quite often with a small pug dog scampering at their heels. A contemporary account noted that whenever they were in Berlin, 'our Fritz' and 'our Louise', as they were known, mixed freely with the children around them, and that 'the pantomime was never so much appreciated, as when the young Prince brought his little sister to share in these childish delights'.[4]

In April 1851 the family received an invitation from Queen Victoria and Prince Albert to stay in England for a few days. The main reason for their doing so was to come and attend the opening of the Great Exhibition at the Crystal Palace in London on the first day of the following month. At this time Louise, who was now known in the family as 'Wiwy' or 'Vivi', was a docile, not to say rather a dull girl of twelve. She made little impression on the company alongside the lively, eager 'Vicky', Victoria, the Princess Royal, her hosts' eldest daughter, who was nearly two years younger than her. When ten-year-old Victoria eagerly showed them around the exhibition, Frederick William was captivated – although his eager, precocious young guest might have been more captivating than anything else – while Louise soon became bored. Maybe she had already had the foresight to appreciate that the traditional role of a German princess was to take no interest in anything outside her family, children, churchgoing and charitable works. Her intellectually-minded mother had learnt the hard way, and soon made it evident that she was much happier when she could leave Berlin and spend time back in Weimar with her original family.

Nevertheless Queen Victoria was sure that the princesses enjoyed each others' company while they were together. Later that month she wrote enthusiastically to her uncle Leopold, King of the Belgians, that

> Never did a visit go off better, we lived all so comfortably & happily together, quite *en famille* & quite at home. Vicky has formed an amazing friendship for that charming Child Vivi, & also for the young Prince; Might this, one day, lead to a union!'[5]

Louise also became friends with Victoria's sister Alice, who was then aged eight. She retained fond memories of this very likeable princess, of whom she wrote some years later,

> was at that time most graceful in appearance – charming, merry and amiable; and though always occupying a subordinate place to her very gifted and distinguished sister, there never was the least semblance of a disagreement .... Our walks and drives together, the life in the schoolroom, the games in the corridors, or in dear old Baron Stockmar's room – these and all the pleasure and enjoyment of being together with the two sisters will ever remain amongst the happiest and most lasting of my recollections.[6]

In May 1853 Augusta, William and Louise visited England a second time. Queen Victoria had given birth to a fourth son, Prince Leopold, one month earlier, and Augusta was invited to be one of the sponsors at his christening.

During her childhood Louise established a close friendship with Rose, the daughter of John Fane, Lord Burghersh, who had been appointed British Minister in Berlin in 1841 for ten years. Educated by Swiss and

German tutors, Rose had seen some of the fighting in the streets during the revolution of 1848. Although she returned to England at the end of her father's period of service in Europe and divided the rest of her life between London and Kent, she and Louise remained friends and continued to correspond together on a regular basis until shortly before her death in February 1921.

The time was coming to think of marriage, and in May 1854 Louise, then aged fifteen, was betrothed to Frederick, Regent of Baden. Queen Victoria was among the first to congratulate Princess Augusta. From her effusive letter, it seemed as if she wished that there had been another Prussian princess in the family who might have become a bride for one of her sons.

> We had already long wished for such a wife for the good Fritz of Baden, and I consider that you yourselves have every reason to be happy at the choice of such a husband for your dear child .... Oh, if only you had such another daughter, a younger! I know of no young girl who would fill a high position so well as Wiwy![7]

Prince Albert also sent his congratulations a few days later, in a rather more reserved fashion, to Prince William. 'If the news that Wiwi is engaged to the Regent of Baden is now true,' he wrote, 'I wish them good luck from my heart.'[8]

Born on 9 September 1826 at Carlsruhe, Frederick (who like his betrothed's brother was always known as 'Fritz' in the family) was the second son of Grand Duke Leopold of Baden, who had married Princess Sophie of Sweden, daughter of King Gustav IV Adolf, in 1819. The couple had eight children, of whom all but one survived infancy. Of the five sons, Louis died within a few months of birth, and the second son, also named Louis, suffered from mental problems. He was followed by Frederick, William and Charles. Alexandrine, the firstborn, married Ernest, Duke of Saxe-Coburg Gotha, the brother-in-law of Queen Victoria, while the other two sisters, Marie and Cecilie, were the youngest of the family.

Frederick and Louis, who was two years his senior, attended Heidelberg University where they studied history and political economy for two years. After a course of military training, Frederick resumed his studies at the University of Bonn. On his father's death in 1852 Louis succeeded to the title, but he was deemed incapable of ruling, and Frederick was appointed Regent in September 1856. Louis lingered for another sixteen months and died in January 1858, aged thirty-three, on which the grand ducal title passed to Frederick.

Baden had been a margraviate at the beginning of the nineteenth century and became a grand duchy in 1806, with an area of about 1,300 square miles (3,400 square kilometres) and a population of 210,000. During the next hundred years it increased in territory and population around fivefold. During the revolutions of 1848 there had been minor disturbances in the state, but without major casualties, and speedily suppressed with assistance from the Prussian forces.

Now a Grand Duchy, Baden was a hereditary monarchy with executive power vested in the Grand Duke, and with legislative authority shared between him and a representative assembly or *Landtag* consisting of two chambers. The upper chamber included all princes of the ruling family of full age, the heads of all the mediatized families, the Archbishop of Freiburg, the President of the Protestant Evangelical

Church of Baden, a deputy from each of the universities and the technical high school, eight members elected by the territorial nobility for four years, three representatives elected by the chamber of commerce, two by that of agriculture, one by the trades, two mayors of municipalities, and eight members (two of them legal functionaries) nominated by the Grand Duke.

Germany in the nineteenth century

The lower chamber included seventy-three popular representatives, of whom twenty-four were elected by the burgesses of certain communities, and forty-nine by rural communities. Every citizen aged twenty-five or over, who had not been convicted and was not a pauper, had a vote. The chambers met at least every two years. The lower chambers were elected for four years, half the members retiring every two years.

Louise and Frederick were married on 20 September 1856 at the Neue Palais Chapel, Potsdam. As first lady of the land, Queen Elizabeth reserved to herself the duty of fastening the crown on the head of the bride.

The Berlin correspondent of *The Times* reported with some cynicism on the proceedings on the city *en fête* and its eagerness to take full commercial advantage of the match, and with no more than faint praise of the royal couple themselves:

> Many of the newspapers of to-day have perpetrated odes to the bridal couple, which, if they bear reading, do certainly not bear translating. Most of the places of public amusement seize on the welcome opportunity to advertise 'several thousand extra lamps' and a variety of attractions for all loyal Berliners, and the proprietor of the advertising columns that stand, not in the newspapers, but at the corners of the different streets, intends to decorate them all to-morrow with garlands and festoons and festal placards, appropriate to the hymeneal solemnity! Apart from all these demonstrations, which are more or less trade puffs, it is impossible to shut one's eyes to the conviction that this people does entertain a lively affection for the Royal family, even here in the capital, the

inhabitants of which have certainly less heart than any other population, and most of all is the Prince of Prussia branch, the family of the King's next eldest brother, the object of this affection, mingled with fervent hopes and confidence in the future. It would indeed be difficult to find even in any secluded private circles two young persons brought up so devoid of the many failings and faults that attach to high birth and Royal expectations as Prince Friedrich Wilhelm and Princess Louisa.

As for the bride and groom, it was remarked of the former rather bluntly that 'she possesses no transcendent beauty, but in its place a sweetness of expression that is worth far more, as indicative of the heart and feeling within,' although the well-known three-quarter portrait of her by Franz Xaver Winterhalter 'is like her in every respect except the hands and arms, which are not well painted, and have been copied from some dairymaid model.' This painting showed her with her head turned half to the left, wearing a low-cut white dress decorated with the Order of Louise, a necklace of pearls, and a wreath of myrtle or orange blossom in her hair. The original is one of several individual portraits of the family in the Pushkin Museum of Fine Art, Moscow, and a copy was presented to Queen Victoria on her birthday in May 1858 by Prince and Princess Frederick William.

A little more graciously, it added that the groom was 'good-looking, with a manly bearing, and the expression of his countenance conveys the strong good sense and firmness of character that he has already evidenced in very trying circumstances', namely his appointment as Regent in place of his sadly deranged brother.[9]

Less cynically and much more warmly, from Scotland Prince Albert wrote to Princess Augusta that he hoped

> you may find calm and rest, that you may be able to bear the separation from your dear daughter. The reflection that it is for her lasting happiness will be the richest source from which you can draw comfort and satisfaction. Our newspapers give so full an account of the festivities in Berlin that we feel as if we had been there with you.[10]

Once they were married, the Grand Duke and Duchess divided their time together between two main homes in Baden. One was the eighteenth-century palace at Carlsruhe. She disliked the stiffness and formality, and always preferred Mainau Castle, a summer residence on Lake Constance, a lake on the Rhine between Germany, Switzerland and Austria. Her father kept her old rooms in the palace at Berlin just as they were during her childhood, ready for her to stay in every time she returned to stay as a welcome guest.[11]

A few weeks after their wedding, Louise discovered that she was expecting her first child and their elder son, named Frederick after his father, was born on 9 July 1857. From a comment which Queen Victoria made in one of her letters to her eldest daughter a couple of years later, he was a good but perhaps none too healthy child, although what illnesses he may have suffered from are not recorded. The Grand Duke, she wrote, was 'quite charming – Il a un charme indicible [indescribable], and Louise is fortunate indeed …. and the little boy must be very intelligent, though not pretty and I fear delicate from what our dear Countess [Blücher, a close personal friend of the Queen and member of Princess Augusta's household] has told me.'[12]

In the second year of their marriage, Louise wrote to the diplomat Alexander von Humboldt of their domestic bliss:

> I recall with gratitude the many occasions when I have ventured to exchange thoughts with you, the many proofs you have continually given me, from my childhood, of your kindly sympathy. It is my warmest wish to see you again now that I am a wife and a mother, to listen with redoubled interest and reverence to your words .... Since we last met, my life has become so much more beautiful, more precious, to me, my happiness is so much richer and deeper than before .... This dear child seems to have brought it to a height undreamt of till now .... If I could but show you the little creature, I know you would delight in it.[13]

Prince Frederick William had returned to Britain in September 1855 as a guest of Queen Victoria and Prince Albert at Balmoral, their home in the Scottish Highlands, during which he became engaged to Victoria, Princess Royal. The news was not altogether popular in Prussia, where most members of the court were sympathetic to Russia. The Crimean war was in progress and Britain and France would emerge victorious, much to the chagrin of many.

The young couple were married at St James's Palace, London, on 25 January 1858. The Grand Duke and Duchess were prevented from attending as his brother Louis was seriously ill, and died at the age of thirty-three, just two days before the ceremony. They were represented by the Grand Duke's younger brother William.

Louise and Victoria had grown up very different in personality. Once she was married and settled at home in Germany, Victoria tried her very best to get on with her, but there was always a sense of none-too-friendly rivalry. The latter's eldest son William, born in January 1859, had to suffer the lifelong handicap of a deformed left hand, arm and shoulder. Moreover, as several members of the Prussian royal family took pleasure in pointing out to his mother, he was smaller and thinner than their babies had been at the same age. Louise, complained Victoria, could not resist boasting that her son was superior; 'hers was bigger the day he was born than mine is now after 8 weeks wh. I take very ill, & wh. surely is hardly possible.'[14]

However Louise could hardly help taking a great interest in her nephew, the boy whom she recognised would be their sovereign one day. Despite his physical handicap, he soon gave signs of being a lively youngster with plenty of personality. When he was barely two years old, Victoria was telling her mother that his devoted aunt 'spoilt him quite dreadfully', and after she had seen him, the governess Mrs Hobbs complained that she was finding it 'very difficult to get him into order again.'[15]

Life in Berlin had its frustrating aspects. Three months after her wedding, Princess Frederick William was writing to Queen Victoria of her irritation at what she had seen; 'no one who has not been here can understand the busy idleness, the active waste of time that goes on. Ask Fritz and Louise of Baden, ask the Princess [Augusta] ....'[16]

At least the sisters-in-law were united by one common factor – the fact that Princess Augusta was so cold towards them and their husbands, although in time she would unbend and take a little more interest in some of the elder grandchildren, but by no means all. It was increasingly evident that family life, such as it was, meant little if anything to her.

At first, there was every chance that Louise and Victoria would be united by another common factor. For some time, Queen Victoria had been considering Louise's sister William as a suitable husband for Alice, the second daughter with whom Louise had struck up such a strong rapport on her first visit to England. Princess Frederick William was not so sure, leading to a reproach from her mother that 'Poor William of Baden is not in your favour, I see'.[17]

When Alice became betrothed to Prince Louis of Hesse in the closing weeks of 1860, Augusta was coldness itself. Not only did she dislike the Hessian family, but as her daughter-in-law perceptively saw, the unhappy wife who had plainly not married for love herself 'takes no interest in anything that has to do with love, as she cannot understand it'. She had not been able to understand how Louise could be fond of Fritz of Baden, or even why Princess Frederick William adored her husband so much.[18] Louise had likewise hoped that Alice would become her brother's bride, and seemed less than pleased when she found it was not to be. Queen Victoria suspected her of spreading lies about Alice and Louis; 'Louise of B. ought indeed to know better, considering my description in two letters of her of the touching love and devotion of the dear young couple ... Louise however wished something different, and that may explain all.'[19]

Just two weeks before this letter was written, on 2 January 1861, King Frederick William IV died. For two or three years he had been living a twilight existence, enfeebled by several increasingly severe

21

strokes. The man who had become a helpless ruin in a bathchair had been for some time unable to recognise anyone around him, and his passing came as a merciful release. William and Augusta were now King and Queen of Prussia.

Yet it made no difference to the antipathy between them, arguing bitterly over everything, much to the distress of the rest of the family. Their daughter-in-law, now Crown Princess, painted a sad portrait of the state of affairs from which it seemed their daughter had been shielded. She said that it literally made her and her husband feel quite unwell. 'Such scenes are most sad to witness anywhere but when it comes to be one's parents it is really enough to make one quite unhappy. I am only thankful that Louise is not present at these discussions.'[20]

At around this time Albert Edward, Prince of Wales, was introduced to Princess Alexandra of Denmark. Queen Victoria had been increasingly preoccupied with finding the right princess for him to marry, and it seemed that in the eldest daughter of Prince Christian, future King of the Scandinavian kingdom, the right bride had been found for him. Because of long-standing and unresolved disputes over the duchies of Schleswig and Holstein, to which Prussia and Denmark both felt they had a claim, the idea was not popular at Berlin. It was rumoured, without foundation, that the family's morals were not beyond question, as Princess Christian was said to have given birth to illegitimate children, and her daughter was a flighty young woman who had had 'flirtations with young officers'. The Crown Princess produced a list of those who had repeated such allegations either verbally or by letter, among whom were the Grand Duke and Duchess of Baden.[21]

If what she said was correct, Louise was apparently not averse to repeating falsehoods where it seemed they might be in the German national interest. Nevertheless such whispers were not enough to prevent the engagement from taking place, and Alexandra duly became the Princess of Wales on her marriage to the British heir in March 1863. Moreover, Louise remained friends with Alice, and she and Frederick would likewise always be on the best of terms with her and Louis during what was to be her sadly short life.

Louise had not known the Prince Consort very well, and had probably not seen him since her second visit to England when she was a girl of fifteen – though they may have met briefly on the Prince's last visit to Germany in the autumn of 1860. Yet when he fell ill at Windsor and died on 14 December 1861, leaving a bereft widow and nine children, she knew from a distance what they were going through.

She was full of admiration for the way in which Alice had stood by Queen Victoria during his illness, and more or less single-handedly taken charge of many of the domestic arrangements. 'Herself filled with intensest sorrow at her beloved father's death - and what a father! what a head of a family! what a friend and adviser to his wife and children! – she at once took into her own hands everything that was necessary in those first dark days of the destruction of that happy home,' she later wrote. Alice, she went on, 'suddenly developed into a wise far-seeing woman, living only for others, and beloved and respected by the highest as well as by the lowest.'[22] After Alice married Louis in July 1862 and settled in Germany, her letters to Queen Victoria contained several references over the years to spending time with the Grand Duke and Duchess at Baden and Mainau, and the latter returning their visits when they came to Darmstadt.

On 7 August 1862, Louise gave birth to a daughter, whom they named Sophie Maria Victoria. The Crown Princess reported to Queen Victoria that the mother was looking well and the child was 'quite enormous'. It did however give her 'a pang of jealousy' when she learned that the baby had suffered a broken right arm during delivery, but it was set again immediately and was perfectly all right as a result.[23] The Crown Princess never ceased to reproach herself for her eldest son's left misshapen arm.

A second son for Louise, Louis William Carl Frederick, was born on 12 June 1865, but never married. With his arrival, the family was now complete. True to her usual form, Queen Augusta took little interest in the family. The Crown Princess bemoaned the state of affairs once again, writing that her mother-in-law hardly ever saw or even enquired after her grandchildren, 'though I believe she is at heart fond of the elder ones'. She had been just the same towards her daughter's family as well, 'and it used to grieve Louise'.[24] Both of them had long since had to accept that the Queen would evidently never change.

Though she took care not to involve herself in political issues or controversies more than possible, the events of Bismarck's Prussia made it impossible for Louise to stand aside all the time. When Otto von Bismarck took power as Prussia's Minister-President and soon demonstrated what he meant when he said that the great questions of the day would not be solved through speeches and majority decisions, but by iron and blood, it was inevitable that family loyalties would become divided.

The Grand Duchy of Baden had always been a fervent supporter of Austria, particularly during the six weeks of the Austro-Prussian war in 1866. When it came to taking up arms, the Grand Duke and the Crown Prince of Prussia found themselves on opposite sides. In spite of this both agreed, as the latter wrote in his diary after leaving the battlefield of the decisive Prussian victory at Königgrätz in the first week of July, that war was 'an appalling thing, and the man who brings it about with a stroke of his pen at the "green table," little reeks [imagines] what he is conjuring with'.[25]

Towards the end of July, shortly before the Battle of Werbach, the second chamber petitioned the Grand Duke to end the war and enter into an offensive and defensive alliance with Prussia. Not surprisingly he had been opposed to the war with Prussia for personal reasons, apart from his hatred of war and bloodshed, but he had to yield to popular resentment at Prussian policy on her claim to the duchies of Schleswig and Holstein, when the ministry resigned. Baden announced her withdrawal from the German Confederation, and on 17 August the minister signed a treaty of peace and alliance with Prussia.

Early the following year the North German Confederation came into existence, excluding the South German states of Baden, Bavaria, Württemberg, and Hesse-Darmstadt. It was however only a temporary compromise. On 9 April the Grand Duke wrote to Prince Chlodwig von Hohenlohe, senior member of the Bavarian *Reichsrat* and shortly to become Bavarian prime minister, that he would 'shrink from no personal sacrifice' in order to promote the union of North and South Germany in one federation.[26]

Throughout the years, the Grand Duke and Duchess continued to take great interest in the development and upbringing of their eldest nephew. In the summer of 1867, when Louise and her husband met William's tutor Georg Hinzpeter, they were immediately impressed with his personality and what they believed was his suitability for the job. The Crown Princess wrote to her husband that Louise and Frederick were 'quite taken' with him and 'have congratulated us on acquiring his services'.[27] It did not become apparent for some time that the man they had chosen was a stern unbending character whose influence on the future Emperor did not turn out for the best.

Despite this, Louise would never be very close to her brother and sister-in-law. She had taken wholeheartedly after her father, and when the family's political differences became evident, the Crown Prince and Princess's liberalism proved a formidable obstacle. King William regularly confided in his daughter about his impatience with the Crown Prince, who did not share his views. His son's opposition, he complained, 'was not only excessive but crowded out every dutiful expression of filial reverence'.[28]

Since her marriage Queen Augusta had always devoted herself unstintingly to good works and charitable organisations, one of the traditional tasks of nineteenth century consorts, and her daughter was keen to follow in her footsteps. As Grand Duchess, Louise played a major role in helping to found the Baden *Frauenverein*, a women's welfare charity which undertook a particular role in providing hospitals and children's homes. For some years she maintained a regular correspondence with Florence Nightingale, who had helped to revolutionise nursing during the conflict between England and Russia less than fifteen years earlier, and was impressed by her knowledge and efficiency. She later said that the Grand Duchess's letters could have been written by any administrator working in the Crimean war.

Shortly after the outbreak of the Franco-Prussian war in July 1870, she met Clara Barton, with whom she would enjoy a lifelong friendship. Miss Barton had previously been a nurse during the American Civil War. While she was travelling in Europe, she helped Louise with the preparation of military hospitals, and gave the Red Cross society invaluable assistance during the conflict. When she was requested by the German authorities and a committee in Strasbourg which had been set up to help the poor and needy, she assisted in general welfare services after the siege of Paris, where she was partly in charge of the public distribution of supplies to the poor. After the war, largely on the suggestion of Louise, Miss Barton was awarded the Golden Cross of Baden by the Grand Duke, and the Iron Cross of Merit by Emperor William I. The experiences she had gained in Europe later bore fruit in her own country when she went on to found the American Red Cross.

During the war against Emperor Napoleon and his empire, the Baden troops fought alongside those of the other German states against France. The Grand Duke proved that he could be very firm in the defence of his Grand Duchy when occasion demanded. After the war, the Bavarian diplomatist Count Bray broached the subject of a possible cession of the towns of Heidelberg and Mannheim to Bavaria. The Grand Duke indignantly refused to consider any such idea, and according to Prince Hohenlohe, spoke his mind firmly to Bray, who 'slunk off like a whipped dog'.[29]

When the German empire was proclaimed in the Salle des Glaces at Versailles in January 1871, the Grand Duke was the first of the German princes to hail his father-in-law as the new Emperor. King William, who had not been at all enthusiastic about his title or imperial status, had been persuaded to accept it by Bismarck and the other Grand Dukes and princes, albeit with bad grace. Having to make the best of an uncongenial situation, shortly before the ceremony he told his son-in-law that he would need to lead the cheers for 'the Emperor of Germany'. Bismarck met the Grand Duke on his way upstairs, and suggested as a compromise that he should simply call for cheers for 'Emperor William'.[30] The exact wording of the new title had been the subject of much argument, but in the end it was decided that 'German Emperor' would be the equivalent of 'Emperor in Germany' and prove less objectionable to the sensitivities of his fellow heads of sovereign states than the more head-of-school-like 'Emperor of Germany'.

For all the splendour with everyone attired in their finery, the declaration of the new imperial status was plainly a rather cheerless occasion, not least thanks to the mood of man who was probably more responsible for the achievement of German unity than anybody else. Putting a brave face on everything, Crown Prince Frederick William noted in his diary that after His Majesty had read aloud a short address to the assembled German sovereigns,

Count Bismarck came forward, looking in the grimmest of humours, and read out in an expressionless, business-like way and without any trace of warmth or feeling for the occasion, the address 'to the German people.' At the words 'Enlarger of the Empire,' I noticed a quiver stir the whole assemblage, which otherwise stood there without a word. Then the Grand Duke of Baden came forward with the unaffected, quiet dignity that is so peculiarly his, and, with uplifted right hand, cried in a loud voice: 'Long

live His Imperial Majesty the Emperor William!'
A thundering hurrah, at the least six times
repeated, shook the room, while the flags and
standards waved above the head of the new
Emperor of Germany and 'Heil di rim
Siegerkranz' rang out. The moment was
extraordinarily affecting, indeed overwhelming,
and was in every way wonderfully fine.[31]

The bad-tempered newly-elevated Emperor might
not have regarded the occasion as 'wonderfully fine',
son, son-in-law and daughter all welcomed the dawn
of empire. Only the latter would live long enough to
see its decline and fall, a little less than fifty years
later.

II

UNDER the new imperial constitution which came into existence in 1871, Baden was an integral part of the German empire. Most governmental matters within the state, among them the army, railways, post office and the conduct of foreign affairs, now passed to the control of Prussia. Thereafter the Grand Duke and his ministers retained only a limited measure of financial control, such as the exclusive right to tax certain goods.

Although the Grand Duke and Duchess and their family were all Lutherans, Baden was one of the foremost Catholic states in Germany, with about two-thirds of their subjects being Roman Catholics. Ever one to suspect anybody who was close to the Emperor and who did not wholeheartedly share his views, particularly members of the family, Bismarck always distrusted Louise as a tool of clerical and Catholic influences. In his view, they had the potential to threaten and undermine the stability of the new German empire.

In June 1859 a concordat had been signed with the Holy See, the ecclesiastical jurisdiction of the Catholic Church in Rome, which placed education under the supervision of the clergy, encouraging the establishment of religious institutes, and resulting in a constitutional struggle through differences with the ruling class. The stage was set for a protracted struggle between secularism and Catholicism. In 1867, when Julius von Jolly was appointed chief minister of

Baden, several constitutional changes were enacted, including guarantees of press freedom, compulsory education for all, and government examinations for all candidates for the priesthood. This last measure was strongly opposed by the Archbishop of Freiburg, head of the Upper Rhenish ecclesiastical province, who had ever since his appointment claimed to exercise the rights of 'the free Church in the free State' that had been set up as one of the fundamental principles of German liberty by the Frankfurt Assembly in 1848. A period of attacks and counter-attacks had followed, culminating in the arrest and arraignment of the Archbishop. The dispute was settled by a compromise, and in a proclamation of April 1860 the Grand Duke declared his allegiance to the Constitution and his desire to rule according to the Diet, while granting the Catholic Church a measure of independence in religious affairs. When the Archbishop died in April 1868 the see remained vacant for several years.

With the proclamation of the dogma of papal infallibility in 1870 and the *Kulturkampf*, the power struggle resulting from Bismarck's attack on the power of the Pope and the Catholic Church from 1873 onwards, there were further difficulties arising from the rebellion of the Roman Catholic priesthood and its collective refusal, supported by the papacy, to submit to Protestant supremacy throughout Germany. Catholic dogmas and doctrines were seen by the German authorities as direct attacks on the modern nation state, and Bismarck, the liberals and the conservatives who represented the interests of orthodox Protestants found the Centre Party's support of the Pope provocative.

The imperial family were divided on the matter, for Emperor William was totally inflexible in his Protestant, anti-Catholic opinions, unlike his wife, their children and their spouses. As the Grand

Duchess of a German state in which the majority of the population were Catholics, it was only to be expected that Louise would take the opposite view. By nature tolerant of both religions, she was at one with the views of her mother that those who followed a different faith and were thus liable to be disadvantaged in the eyes of the official world for this very reason were in effect a persecuted minority. When she was in Berlin, she saw it as a duty to rally to the cause of those who defended them. As for affairs in her husband's grand duchy, only after the fall of Jolly's ministry was Baden reconciled with Rome, but the archbishopric of Freiburg was left vacant until 1882.

In February 1874 a motion brought forward by some of the deputies from Alsace and Lorraine resulted in uproar in the *Reichstag* after one of their leaders, Deputy Teusch, asked permission to address the House in French, on the grounds that he was more fluent in that language than in German. As his request was contrary to the business regulation of the assembly, his request was refused. There was further anger when he proposed that a decree from the *Reichstag* that the population of Alsace and Lorraine, 'which had been incorporated into the Empire by the treaty of Frankfort without being consulted upon the point, should be called upon to record its vote on the incorporation'.[1] The deputies of Alsace-Lorraine would not unanimously accept the motion. The Bishop of Strasbourg, Dr Bass, considered it his duty to declare that neither he nor the Catholics of Alsace-Lorraine intended to call in question the legality of the treaty of Frankfurt, nor the incorporation of those provinces into the German Empire. At this point the unrest subsided, but even so a feeling remained that justice was not being done.

Bismarck's suspicions of Louise and his fears that she might try and interfere in matters of state deepened when she interceded with her father, now Emperor, on behalf of the oppressed Catholics of Alsace, whom she believed were being discriminated against. As a very rare if not unique attempt at intervention in political matters on her part, this request for clemency was one that the Chancellor did his best to see came to nothing.

Some fifty years later, shortly after her death, it was commented on that according to the reminiscences of Bismarck's contemporaries, he often had reason to complain of the influence that the Grand Duchess attempted to exercise over her father at this time. The statesman was notorious for seeing enemies around him where none may have existed, but as she was the daughter and the sister-in-law of two women at court whom he regarded as threats, he did not hesitate to try and blacken her as an intriguer, or 'the instrument of her mother .... in weaving petticoat intrigues round the old Emperor'.[2] Fond as the sovereign was of his daughter, he would not betray what were to him the principles of a lifetime, and it all came to nothing.

Like so many of her contemporaries among the princesses, Louise did not regard herself as a political animal. She fully appreciated that for much of the time, her main duty was to support her parents at Berlin in their social round. Doing so had become almost purgatory for the Crown Prince and Princess, who found the everlasting *soirées* and parties, the late hours and suffocating heat in the palaces, utterly exhausting. The Emperor and Empress, the Crown Princess wrote to her mother, were 'most marvellously constituted; the more of this kind of thing is going on the better they seem to feel and look – it is quite astonishing.'[3]

Even if she did not live solely for pleasure, Louise was happy to accept it as a matter of course, unlike her sister-in-law who bitterly resented every moment of such an existence. She also found herself supporting her father under fire one day in May 1878, when they were driving along the Unter den Linden in a carriage and an unemployed plumber, Max Hödel, fired at his sovereign, but missed and killed a bystander instead. He was captured, put on trial and executed later that year.

A readiness to embrace the status quo also applied to Louise's attitude towards the control which Bismarck, who had been recently promoted from Prussian Minister-President to the post of German Chancellor, exerted over the German empire. The Grand Duke of Baden had the utmost respect for Bismarck, whom he credited with the unification of Germany and the creation of a strong power, and he always enjoyed excellent relations with his parents-in-law.

His eldest nephew Prince William, the future Emperor, generally found his company and that of his aunt Louise more congenial than that of his own parents, with whom his political differences were particularly pronounced. She had always taken a keen interest in his welfare and education. When he was a student at Bonn she was one of his most trusted confidantes, always ready to discuss weighty religious matters and other subjects with him. Like almost everybody from her generation, she was happy to indulge and flatter the future Emperor. In his second volume of memoirs, which would be written (or ghost-written) during the early years of his exile in Holland during the 1920s, he recalled fondly that his aunt

> possessed considerable political ability and a great gift for organisation, and she understood

excellently how to put the right men in the right place and how to employ their strength serviceably for the general benefit. Although it was not always recognised, she had learned admirably to combine the Prussian element with the Baden character, and she developed into a model sovereign princess.[4]

During Prince William's time at Bonn as a student, he made very few close friends, as might have been expected with one of his rank. One of them who could be counted among that number was Louise's elder son Frederick, who was less than two years older than him. The Crown Princess knew which of them was the stronger character, writing to her husband that their son 'has always tended to order his cousin about, which is not difficult given the weak will & the meagre talent of the latter'.[5] William shone a more cheerful light on their relationship, writing to his aunt the following year that 'Fritz and I get along wonderfully and have already had a few good chats with one another.'[6]

Much as Louise loved and admired her nephew, this kindness did not initially extend to her nephew's wife Augusta Victoria ('Dona'), whom he married in Berlin in February 1881. At the time of Dona's arrival in the capital, Louise was very impressed with her, realised she would make an ideal husband for William, and called her 'wholly delightful, sweet, natural and uninhibited'.[7] Yet within weeks of the wedding Dona was facing a barrage of criticism from her husband's family, and though the situation improved in time, she would never forget it. By far the worst offender of all, she would later tell her own daughter Victoria Louise, Duchess of Brunswick, was Louise, Grand Duchess of Baden. Full of airs and graces, the woman who had become her aunt by marriage did not hesitate to overwhelm her with instructions as to what a princess in her position ought to do, and demanded complete obedience.

In 1879 Louise's daughter Victoria, then aged seventeen, was introduced to Gustav, Crown Prince of Sweden and Norway, while he was taking part in the military manoeuvres at Strasbourg. Two years older than her, Gustav was the son of King Oscar II and Queen Sophie. There had long since been a close affinity between Germany and Sweden, with a close family connection in that Sophie, the previous Grand Duchess of Baden and Louise's mother-in-law, had been a daughter of King Gustav IV Adolf, who lost his throne in the revolution of 1809. Another marriage uniting the royal house of Bernadotte in Sweden and the grand ducal family of Baden was deemed appropriate, and later that year it was announced that the young couple were betrothed. To prepare the bride for her future, a Swedish tutor was sent to Carlsruhe to instruct her in Swedish language and history.

On 20 September 1881, the twenty-fifth anniversary of the wedding of the Grand Duke and Duchess of Baden, the bride and groom were married at Carlsruhe. As if keen not to show too much enthusiasm, the German correspondent of *The Times* noted with some cynicism that it was

> Conceivable that the silver wedding of their ruler and the marriage of his only daughter should have had the effect of rousing the people of Baden from the phlegmatic monotony to which as second-rate provincials, contributing less than half an army corps to the Imperial host, they are ordinarily doomed. In the old gambling days, when reckless Russian Princes and

prodigal English plutocrats rushed to Baden-Baden to win or lose a fortune at *rouge et noir*, the Duchy was never ill off for gossip at least, if not excitement, but virtue has now deposed vice at that fashionable watering-place – mainly, it may be remarked, owing to the initiative of Prince Bismarck when Prussian member of the Frankfort Diet – and virtue has brought obscurity and dullness.[8]

At the ceremony Emperor William, it was observed, was 'looking the picture of bronzed and vigorous health', while Empress Augusta, now an invalid confined to a wheelchair, was well enough to attend but not to stand. As well as the groom's parents, several German royalty were among those present, among representatives from Russia, and also Crown Prince Frederick of Denmark. At the time it was widely interpreted as a sign that Sweden belonged to the German sphere of influence in Europe. The match was popular among the Swedish people, who called Victoria 'the Vasa princess' because of her descent from the old Vasa dynasty which had ruled Sweden in the sixteenth and seventeenth centuries. She received a warm welcome when she made her first entry into Stockholm with her husband in the first week of October.

Nevertheless it did not turn out to be a happy marriage. Guests and observers at the ceremony had not failed to notice that bride and groom appeared very unenthusiastic about one another, and certainly gave no impression of being in love with each other; 'the Prince seemed sullen and angry; the Princess cold and almost antagonistic!'[9] Perhaps oblivious to any signs of mutual antipathy on either side, the marriage had been eagerly welcomed by both families, who may have been unconcerned or even unaware that Gustav was bisexual.

Within a few years, they had a family of three sons. Gustav Adolf, who would succeed his father on the throne, was born in 1882, William in 1884, and Eric in 1889. Victoria suffered intense post-natal depression after the birth of the first, if not all three, partly as a result it was believed of being treated with mercury and other heavy medication during what proved to be difficult pregnancies. Before long she took to spending the winter months of each year outside Sweden. This may have been partly on medical advice, especially after a severe bout of pneumonia in 1889, and partly because she was keen not to have to spend too much time with a husband who she discovered was unnaturally fond of good-looking male courtiers and other company. As a Crown Princess with a strong will of her own, she was unwilling to forgo any luxuries which she thought were her due, and the expense of her visits abroad were often the subject of conflict between her and her frugal parents-in-law, who doubtless thought she was a hypochondriac, as well as failing to do her proper duty as a wife and mother.

A joint holiday for husband and wife to Egypt to try and mend their relationship around ten years into their marriage did nothing to restore marital harmony, allegedly due to her sudden fondness for the company of a male courtier. In view of the strained relationship with her husband and his fondness for male company, she could hardly have been blamed. However it did not help where her family were concerned, nor do anything to counteract her increasing unpopularity with the people of Sweden.

Victoria had inherited the artistic talents of the Hohenzollern family, such as they were, and she grew up to be an accomplished amateur photographer, painter, and sculptor. Her travels throughout Egypt and Italy allowed her scope to take photographs, experiment with various new photo-developing techniques, and paint. She was also a keen musician, a lover of the music of Beethoven and Schubert above all, and in her earlier days she had turned the music for Franz Liszt when he played at court concerts in Berlin. She was an excellent pianist, and was reputed to be able to play through the complete *Ring of the Nibelung* by Wagner without needing to refer to the music. As a lover of the outdoor life, she was also a skilled and enthusiastic rider.

She was every inch a Hohenzollern. Very proud of her family heritage, very haughty and always conscious of her royal position, she was furious when her brother-in-law Oscar had the temerity to fall in love with her lady-in-waiting, Ebba Munck. In 1885 Oscar spent some time in Amsterdam for medical reasons. Victoria and Ebba both visited him there, and he and Ebba fell in love. When he declared to the family that he intended to marry her, they were all shocked. She was immediately dismissed from her post, and he was ordered not to see her for another two years, in the hope that their feelings would eventually cool. It was no use, for after the two-year period he told them that he had still not changed his mind. At length they gave way to his determination, and consented to their marriage on condition that his younger brothers should sign a solemn and binding agreement that they would never enter into similar marriages.

It was realised that the Swedish royal family had no choice but to make the best of a difficult situation. On 21 January 1888, a ball was arranged at the Royal palace in Stockholm where the young couple were permitted to dance with each other, and eight days later their engagement was formally announced. Although the King, Queen and their family did not try to put on a false show of enthusiasm, the betrothal was popular with the public, who seemed to welcome it as a more democratic marriage alliance, saying that a bridge, 'the Munck bridge', had been placed between the people and the royal house. Perhaps they were aware that their Crown Prince and his German wife were not exactly well-matched, and that a morganatic marriage pursued in the face of official disapproval was more likely to be a genuine love match.

When the bride and groom left Stockholm to travel to England for their wedding, a large crowd gathered at the station to wave them off and wish them well. The ceremony took place on 15 March at St Stephen's Church, Bournemouth, with Queen Sophie, the groom's brothers Carl, Duke of Västergotland and Eugene, Duke of Närke, and despite her disapproval of the match, the Crown Princess in attendance, alongside the parents of the bride. The couple were given the titles of Prince and Princess Bernadotte that same day. Seven years later the prince was also granted the hereditary title Count of Wisborg by his uncle Adolf, Grand Duke of Luxembourg, previously Duke of Nassau.

Though Louise had not been particularly close to her mother in childhood, once she was an adult the situation between them improved. They were united in their hopes for Louise's elder son. During the first few weeks of 1883 mother and daughter both thought that there was every chance Louise's elder son Frederick would marry Elizabeth (Ella) of Hesse. She was the second daughter of the widowed Grand Duke Louis, whose wife Alice, Queen Victoria's second daughter, had become and remained such a good friend of Louise, but had died from diphtheria in 1878. Empress Augusta had never forgiven Alice after the controversial theologian Dr Strauss dedicated one of his books to her, and about a week after her death remarked callously at a tea party that it was just as well for her children that she had died as, 'like all English Princesses, she was a complete atheist!'[10] It seems unlikely that her daughter shared such a narrow-minded view. However, when Ella made it clear that she intended to marry Grand Duke Serge Alexandrovich of Russia, one of the younger brothers of Tsar Alexander III, Louise thought her family had been snubbed, and relations between her and the Crown Princess became more distant still.

'You will have heard that there was some little disagreeableness here – between Louis and the Baden family,' the Crown Princess wrote to her mother in March.

> I will not touch upon it because it is no business of mine. I only think that they were a little hard on Louis, and I felt very sorry for him. I hope all feeling of annoyance will soon pass off on all sides.[11]

Although she disliked Russia and did not look with any joy to the idea of her granddaughter marrying into the Romanovs, Queen Victoria fully agreed that it had been a little unjust of Louise and Fritz of Baden to accuse Grand Duke Louis of any want of openness.

> The only chance was to wait – instead of which Louise and Fritz hurried it on, and Louis could not in justice to his child help telling her that others had wished to marry her – when she declared she would not accept poor Fritz of B. junior. Perhaps he did not make himself agreeable or make his wishes very evident?[12]

Later in 1883 the family became fiercely divided over the possibility of a marriage between the Crown Prince and Princess's second daughter Victoria and Alexander of Battenberg, sovereign prince of Bulgaria. The good-looking Alexander was deemed a thoroughly eligible bachelor, and two of his brothers, Louis and Henry, had recently married a granddaughter, Victoria of Hesse, and a daughter, Beatrice, of Queen Victoria. However, as one of the sons of a morganatic marriage between Prince Alexander of Hesse and Countess Julie von Hauke, a former lady-in-waiting at the Russian court, and also as one who had incurred the enmity of Tsar Alexander III, whom Emperor William and Bismarck were determined not to offend, any such match was quite out of the question.

Louise unhesitatingly sided with her parents and nephew William. She agreed with them that such a *mésalliance* was quite unworthy of the Hohenzollern dynasty. William found her a valuable ally, not only with regard to the Battenberg controversy, but also in assuming an attitude of defiance in general disputes with his parents.

Any disappointment that Louise's son Frederick might have felt at being 'snubbed' by Ella of Hesse did not last long. On 20 September 1885 he married Princess Hilda of Nassau, daughter of Adolf, Grand Duke of Luxembourg and Duke of Nassau. At the time of the betrothal in April that year, much was made by the press of the political significance of the forthcoming match, as the bride-to-be's father had seen his territory annexed by Prussia after the defeat of 1866. By coincidence son, daughter and parents all celebrated their weddings on the very same day of the year.

By this time Louise's own parents, the elderly Emperor and Empress, were in poor health. The Crown Prince was distrusted at court because of his wife's influence, and as a 'good German', Louise took it upon herself to spend more of her time supporting them. They made no secret of the fact that she was clearly their favourite, and the Crown Princess strongly resented the authoritarian manner of the sister-in-law who had once been so good and trusted a friend. 'The Empress's caprices, supported by Louise of Baden, are a very great misfortune for us,'[13] she wrote pointedly to Queen Victoria in the autumn of 1886.

Early the following year Louise came to Berlin so she could help to organise festivities for the Emperor's forthcoming ninetieth birthday. It was a role for which she was well suited, especially as Crown Prince Frederick William was sounding unnaturally hoarse, and beginning to display the symptoms of what would prove to be his final illness, cancer of the larynx. After the birthday banquet on 22 March 1887 she stayed ostensibly to help their father, but also so that she could consult with the doctors and act as a self-appointed press agent on behalf of the court at Berlin.

Thanks to her, several articles about her brother's health reached the press without her asking or consulting him or the Crown Princess. Keen, or rather determined to try and exert some control over affairs wherever she could, she made a habit of regularly summoning the doctors so they could give her direct information on the state of her brother's health. The Crown Princess was infuriated by what she saw as wanton interference at such a delicate time. 'Dear Louise of Baden questions & talks me to death till I nearly turn rude!',[14] she wrote angrily to Queen Victoria. Despite some differences of outlook in the early days of the latter's marriage, by now Louise and Dona had long since been reconciled. Moreover Louise had become part of the reactionary, anti-Semite movement which influenced Prince William and Princess Augusta Victoria in championing the notorious court chaplain Adolf Stöcker.

Adding to the general ill-feeling among the family was Louise's taking sides with the view at court that her brother's second daughter Victoria should not be allowed to marry Alexander von Battenberg, who had until recently been sovereign Prince of Bulgaria. Victoria's elder siblings and her grandparents in Berlin were united in their opposition to the idea, with the ageing but still indomitable Empress Augusta particularly clamorous. Even after Alexander was forced to abdicate after a Russian coup in 1886, Crown Princess Frederick William still hoped that the marriage would come about.

While Louise was staying with her parents at Berlin around the time of the Emperor's ninetieth birthday celebrations in March 1887, she assisted the Empress in preparing a codicil to his last will and testament. Now in increasingly poor health after several minor strokes, it had become apparent that he was unlikely to live much longer. It stated that if Princess Victoria defied them and married the former Prince of Bulgaria, she and her mother, the Crown Princess, would both be disinherited and would therefore receive nothing.

Louise was unhesitatingly on their side in all matters to do with the family. As speculation continued to mount regarding the Crown Prince's state of health, she called a meeting of all the doctors and demanded a report on his condition. Like the rest of the court, she did not trust the Crown Princess or the British laryngologist, Sir Morell Mackenzie, who had been put in charge of the case. He and the Crown Princess clung to the hope that, with careful treatment and sufficient rest, the patient would make a full recovery.

Their hopes were soon to be dashed. By the end of the year, it was evident that the Crown Prince was seriously if not mortally ill. On medical advice he spent the winter months far away from Berlin in the hope that the warmer climate of San Remo, on the Riviera, would give him some chance of recovery, or at least prolong his life a little further. Nevertheless, some at court in Berlin feared that he might not outlive his father.

1888 was to prove a year of great sadness for the family, for Louise lost three of her closest male relatives within four months, two of them long before their time. On 23 February her younger unmarried son Louis died suddenly at the age of twenty-two, officially from an inflammation of the lungs.[15] It was however rumoured at the time that he had been killed in a duel.

Everyone expected that the enfeebled ninety-year-old Emperor would follow him very soon. Louise was among those ready to take her place in the hushed family vigil around his bed in the palace at Berlin early the following month, as his strength was ebbing. By the first week of March, everyone knew that there was little hope left. The Empress, also very frail herself by now, was wheeled up close to the bed, so that her left hand was resting on it and she could hold the Emperor's left hand. In front of her stood Louise, who found it necessary to act as an intermediary in their conversation, for the Empress's voice was by now so weak that she had some difficulty in making herself understood. At times the Emperor talked to them, particularly about the political situation and the threat of conflict between Germany and other nations, particularly France. His mind seemed to be wandering, and at one stage he said that if he should have to go to war, he would not be afraid to do so.

On the evening of 8 March, when he fell back exhausted, Louise told him gently, 'You have told us so much that was interesting, perhaps you would like to rest a little now.' 'I have not time for that now,' he told her, and continued talking.[16] Overnight, he became so weak that everyone prepared for the worst. A story which may or may not be sentimental legend was told that, at a very last signal from him, Louise went into an adjoining room to fetch a miniature portrait of his long-dead first love, Elise Radziwill. She placed it in his hands just before he drew his final breath.

To his daughter, the Emperor had bequeathed a copy of the New Testament, published in 1818, with a bejewelled crucifix of lapis lazuli affixed to the cover. It had been presented to Elise Radziwill by her mother, and the cross by the then Prince William, on the occasion of her confirmation in 1820, and left to him when she died of consumption in 1824. Louise accordingly left this long-cherished family keepsake in her will to her nephew William, who became Crown Prince on his grandfather's death.

William I, German Emperor

Augusta, German Empress

King Frederick William IV of Prussia

Princess Louise of Prussia, 1856

Louise and Frederick, Grand Duke and Duchess of Baden,
at the time of their engagement, 1856

Prince and Princess Frederick William of Prussia, c.1860

Louise, Grand Duchess of Baden, in the early years of her marriage

The Grand Duke and Duchess of Baden with the Crown Prince and Princess of Prussia, in mourning for King Frederick William IV, 1861

Frederick, Grand Duke of Baden, c.1865

The Grand Duchess of Baden and her daughter Victoria,
c.1866

The Grand Duchess of Baden and her son Louis, c.1870

The Grand Duchess of Baden and her children, c.1871

Clara Barton, who assisted the Grand Duchess in nursing work during the Franco-Prussian war

The proclamation of the German Empire at Versailles, January 1871, with Emperor William I flanked by Crown Prince Frederick William and Grand Duke Frederick of Baden, with Prince Otto von Bismarck on the right

Alice, Grand Duchess of Hesse and the Rhine, c.1875

Crown Prince Frederick William of Prussia, c.1880

2. AUNT TO THE EMPEROR

I

LOUISE'S brother, who took the name of Emperor Frederick III, was destined to reign for a mere three months, or ninety-nine days. For much of the time he was in sheer agony. His voice had gone completely, and he could only communicate with others by writing on a pad of paper. In San Remo when the news was brought to him of his father's death he, the new Empress and their suite made preparations to return to the bitter cold and snows of Berlin and arrived back that same week, but he was unable to attend his father's funeral and had to content himself with sorrowfully watching the procession from the palace window.

When it became apparent in June that the Emperor had only a few days left, it was the Grand Duke and Duchess of Baden who prepared the Dowager Empress Augusta for the approaching sad news. On 15 June he passed away at the age of fifty-six.

Louise attended his funeral with their mother, who had been helpless and confined to her wheelchair for some years. Notwithstanding the bitter family divisions, like the rest of the court, Louise soon showed herself to be a faithful supporter of her nephew, now Emperor William II.

Though any illusions her sister-in-law, who now became known as the Empress Frederick, may have had about Louise's better nature had long since been dispelled, she still nursed some faint hope that the once-liberal Fritz of Baden might prove to be her ally. It was in vain, for as she wrote to Queen Victoria in October 1888 the Grand Duke had 'completely changed in politics', while Louise declared that 'William behaves so wonderfully well in every way' because he 'walks in the way of his grandfather'.[1] She had expected no better from her sister-in-law. Some three months earlier she had written with bitterness that the reigning party in Prussia seemed anxious to wipe out all traces of her husband's reign, 'and the Empress Augusta and Louise of Baden refuse to see all this as it is, that they are really blinded to these facts.'[2]

Louise's devotion to her mother was now the latter's only close family tie in the next generation, and she was very fond of her two surviving Baden grandchildren. Relations between mother and daughter had once been less than close, if not exactly distant. It was noticeable that they became warmer with the years, particularly after Empress Augusta's mobility and therefore social life were increasingly curtailed by ill-health and old age.

The Grand Duchess of Baden and her family always looked up to her with reverence, although the children and grandchildren inevitably felt that she belonged to a different age from theirs. A new generation had come to the front, and a leap had been made from a nonagenarian ruler who had clung to the ways of an age long since past, to a young one eager to find himself a role on the European stage. The premature death of Emperor Frederick had created an all too sudden bridge from one era to the next, and the general attitude of the family towards the Dowager Empress, now in her late seventies, was less that of respect for her mental powers, than compassion for her failing physical state. By now she divided most of her time between Baden-Baden, Carlsruhe, the island of Mainau and Coblenz. She was increasingly dependent on Louise, who had become more and more attached to her mother after the recent deaths in the family circle that had brought them so much sorrow.

In the second week of December 1889 Empress Augusta returned to Berlin for Christmas, which she planned to spend with her daughter and son-in-law. At the time she was suffering from a heavy cold, although preparations in the household still ran in accordance with her instructions.

Over the winter a severe epidemic of influenza, the most virulent that had been known for many years, was raging throughout Europe. The Grand Duke and Duchess of Baden and several members of the household were among those laid low for a few days by the virus. Empress Augusta managed to avoid it for a while, and as the new year of 1890 dawned she appeared her usual self. On new year's day she received the Emperor and Empress, who wanted to be the first to offer their congratulations and greet her at the beginning of another year. That evening she entertained a party of generals and courtiers who had served her and the late Emperor William to dinner, and a few days later she was present at a meeting of Red Cross workers.

On 6 January she felt unwell and took to her bed. When she showed symptoms of the fever, her doctors knew that in her weakened state it would surely be a relief to her if her sufferings were to cease. Her physician Dr Velten, and an assistant, Dr Schliep, immediately took charge, while Louise spent the night by her bed. At one stage her mother awoke, saw her sitting alongside, and whispered, 'Good child!'[3] As long as the fever was under control, the doctors said that there was no immediate danger, though the age of the patient and her weak state gave them cause for grave concern.

She became worse during the night, when an alarming rise in temperature suggested her condition was critical. From the small hours of Tuesday morning, her breathing seemed uneven and her strength was failing. By then she was only conscious from time to time, and relations gathered as it was possible that she would not last another night.

By late afternoon the doctors admitted that the end was drawing near. The Emperor and Empress, the Grand Duke and Grand Duchess of Baden, the Hereditary Prince and Princess of Saxe-Meiningen and his wife had not left the bedside for some hours, and family members in the adjoining rooms were now called in. Her voice choking with sobs, Louise bent over her mother as she asked her to convey her loving greetings to the dear ones gone before. Then the doctor announced that the Empress Augusta had breathed her last.

Full of sympathy for Louise, the Empress Frederick, who was in Italy at the time and hurried back for the funeral, asked Queen Victoria if she would offer her the Order of Victoria & Albert. It had been conferred on the late Empress and her insignia should by rights now be returned to the Queen. However the Empress suggested that it would be a compliment to the memory of the Empress Augusta if it was to be offered to her daughter instead. She told the Queen that Louise was 'sorely stricken & feels her mother's death very much; so I venture to plead your giving her her mother's order.'[4] She might have been less charitably disposed had she known that a suggestion by Louise was partly if not largely responsible for helping to deprive her sister-in-law of her rightful role as head of the two most important German charitable societies, posts that had been held by the Empress Augusta. Instead the position went to Empress Augusta Victoria, who was admittedly Empress Consort but had none of the Empress Frederick's experience or knowledge.

In March 1890, after increasing differences and angry exchanges with the young Emperor, Prince Bismarck resigned as German Chancellor. Initially the Grand Duke of Baden thought that in spite of his advancing years – he was seventy-three at the time of the Emperor's accession – his young master 'needs the Chancellor for the present, to bring forward Army Bills.'[5] But they would soon learn that nobody was indispensable. One of the factors that contributed to his downfall was a dispute over the Emperor's labour policy, and in a farewell interview with the Grand Duke, the veteran statesman reproached him bitterly for having connived at his fall by supporting his nephew's idea.

The Grand Duke had never been anything but a great admirer of Bismarck and his policies. Yet he had been aware that the Emperor was gradually losing patience with the architect of the German empire. When he found it necessary to repudiate the idea that he might have been responsible for the Chancellor's downfall, the latter 'became rude' and Frederick, declaring that he could not tolerate his language, abruptly terminated their conversation. However, not wishing to part from him in anger, he said he would bid the great man farewell with the words, 'Long live the Emperor and the Empire'.[6] In spite of their respect for the politician and their agreement with his policies, there was never any doubt in the views of the Grand Duke and Duchess that their nephew had been well within his rights to call for the elderly man's resignation.

Two years later when the Empress Frederick's third daughter Sophie, was married to Constantine, Crown Prince of the Hellenes, and living in Athens, she found her mother's constant questions a little trying, and innocently compared her to the Grand Duchess of Baden. As no great admirer of her sister-in-law, the Empress found this anything but a compliment:

> I am <u>much</u> flattered to be compared to Aunt Louise of Baden! The difference, you see, is that she asks questions because it is a habit and she cannot help it, because it is her way of making conversation, and because she loves meddling in other people's affairs and making herself important.[7]

It was not only the Empress who found her sister-in-law and her manner unnecessarily imperious. After his grandmother Empress Augusta's death, the Emperor had decided that his only surviving brother Henry and his wife Irene ought to be allowed to take over the royal palace Unter den Linden, which had been the former residence of Emperor William I for so many years.

Louise felt that as their daughter she had a prior claim on the property which should be considered as more important than that of her nephew. When she was approached by the Emperor on the matter, she refused to remove her parents' furniture or to give up her own right of residence. Henry, his wife Irene and their family lived in another wing of the palace for a while, but because of her uncompromising attitude they never really felt at home there. In 1893 the Emperor chose another Berlin residence, the Niederländisches Palace for his brother and sister-in-law, but still the matter of Unter den Linden remained unresolved because of Louise's attitude. While the Emperor was in effect the head of the family, his aunt insisted on having her own way and was not slow to put forward what she considered a prior claim on the properties that had formerly been owned by her parents.

Although Louise had generally been just as commanding as her mother, always keen to have her own way, relations between her and her sister-in-law gradually improved. This may in part have been a reaction against the behaviour of the Emperor, about whom they had soon become rather disillusioned. Members of the young sovereign's family and foreign diplomats were increasingly critical of him, some even beginning to share the opinion of their cousins in England and Darmstadt that he was alarmingly inconsistent, arrogant and possibly not altogether sane.

Within a couple of years of his accession, they were proving less supportive than they had been at the start. They complained that he was all too often taking 'overhasty action' and losing that support with the German public that he had had at the start of his reign. While they had hoped for the best, and expected that everything would turn out well, they were soon less sanguine. In October 1890 the Grand Duke met Field-Marshal Alfred von Waldersee, chief of the imperial general staff and a former devoted admirer of the Emperor. Waldersee confided his grave concerns about the Emperor, which confirmed what the Grand Duke had heard from other sources. He said he had discussed the problem with Count Leo von Caprivi, who had succeeded Bismarck as chancellor earlier that year, and expressed a fear that 'pushy people might easily acquire influence these days'. Caprivi told him solemnly that that was already the case. They believed that the Emperor was far too impulsive, if not actually unstable, and a poor judge of character.

While they were reluctant to lose faith in their nephew, four years later their views had hardly changed. Waldersee, who had become a close friend, spent an evening with them in the summer of 1894. As a couple, he told them, they had always set 'an outstanding example of devotion to duty and of regal dignity', and it was not surprising that they had grave reservations about the conduct of the Emperor. Louise told him that, as far as her nephew was concerned, she strongly deprecated 'the lack of imperial dignity which one cannot fail to notice if one has but seen the daily life of the Kaiser and his relations with his entourage'. While she had always recognized his best qualities such as his quick understanding and his knowledge on so many different subjects, she was shocked by his volatility and hastiness, and thought that his many ill-considered decisions were an inevitable consequence. If she ever wondered about his mental stability or lack of it, she was not the only one.

Grand Duke Frederick singled out for particular criticism his nephew's evident craving for pleasure and lack of seriousness. Not long before, the Emperor had come to visit his uncle, but went out shooting every morning and spent no more than half an hour in serious conversation with him about matters of state. The Grand Duke was especially annoyed that the Emperor had apparently taken a decision that August on a particularly important religious question of the day, on the return of the Redemptorist Order, a Roman Catholic missionary organisation, to Germany, at Kiel - during a hasty and grudgingly-given fifteen-minute audience while he was there to enjoy the delights of the annual regatta week.[8] To him it suggested a very questionable order of priorities ill-befitting one of the most powerful monarchs in Europe. He and Louise both felt this unashamed devotion to his sporting enjoyment boded ill for the future.

Yet as senior members of the Emperor's family, their influence still counted for something. When Caprivi resigned his position in October 1894, it was largely on the Grand Duke's advice that Chlodwig zu Hohenlohe-Schillingsfürst, a distant cousin of Queen Victoria, was appointed to replace him as Chancellor. Nevertheless it had gradually dawned on Louise and her husband that Emperor William II was not the flawless young man they had believed him to be, and that the mother whom he and official Germany had so maligned at around the time of the untimely death of Emperor Frederick had been misjudged. From around this time onwards, there was an evident healing in relations between the Grand Duke and Duchess and the Empress Frederick. In the autumn of 1895 the latter was invited to stay with them at Carlsruhe on the occasion of the unveiling of a statue to the memory of her husband, and afterwards she wrote to Sophie that 'Uncle Fritz and Aunt Louise are most kind and try to make me feel at home.'[9]

Some four years later, all three of them met at Carlsruhe station when the Empress was on her way through Baden, and she wrote to Queen Victoria that she thought they both looked lined and old, but were 'very kind & much disturbed that I was not well!'[10] Though the Empress was the youngest of the three, she was already seriously ill. After a fall from her horse about eighteen months earlier she had never been the same again, and was later diagnosed with cancer of the spine. She would be the first to pass away, with less than fifteen months to live.

Louise and her husband lived to enjoy a more healthy and contented old age than her brother and his wife ever knew. In his memoirs the Chancellor Bernhard von Bülow noted that the Grand Duchess

> profoundly understood her husband's greatness, [and] supplemented his character in the happiest manner. I do not think that even patriarchal Germany produced a ruling Princess who did her duty as the mother of her people in a more exemplary manner than Grand Duchess Louise.[11]

After the statesman had christened SS *Deutschland* at Stettin in January 1900, and made a speech declaring that Germany had to take her place in the world as a leading sea power, she telegraphed to him:

> I cannot resist telling you what a grateful echo the patriotic, moderate and enthusiastic words of the speech you made yesterday in Stettin found within me.[12]

Louise had not maintained her early connections with her British in-laws, and as a proud German maybe she had no good reason to do so. All the same, the illness and death of Queen Victoria at Osborne House on the Isle of Wight in January 1901 evidently stirred some feelings in her of the more carefree childhood days when she had been a guest of the Queen and Prince Albert as a young girl at the time of the Great Exhibition. During the celebrations taking place to mark the bicentenary of the Hohenzollern monarchy that same month, the Emperor was warned that his 'unparalleled grandmama' was seriously ill. He understood that the end was approaching, and therefore cancelled all his plans to go to England at once so he could go and join the family at her deathbed at Osborne. Five days after she passed away on 22 January, he celebrated his birthday – in very subdued fashion – as he stayed in England to attend her funeral, which took place at Windsor on 2 February. Louise wrote him a letter in which she sent him her best wishes for this happy forty-second birthday, which made her own feelings clear as she related to him having played his part

> so wonderfully a grandson and son, accompanying that great life, whose passing we all mourn, to its end. I feel deeply affected; for me it brings to a close a wealth of precious memories of childhood and youth, beginning 50 years ago in 1851. What an uplifting time this must be for you, no doubt reminiscent of 1888. God bless you in all that you are living through over there, for it is of such great significance both now and for the future.[13]

Just over six months later, on 5 August, the Empress Frederick died. Aged sixty, she had been bedridden for some months, in constant agony from her illness. The Grand Duke and Duchess did not attend the official funeral ceremony eight days later at Potsdam, but they paid tribute to their sister-in-law with a memorial service at Badenweiler, held by an English chaplain and attended by a large congregation.

In April 1902 the fiftieth anniversary of the Grand Duke's accession was marked with tributes in the *Reichstag* in Berlin, where the President gave expression to the feelings of the deputies, who stood up in their places as a mark of respect. The Emperor, the King of Württemberg, and several other German princes went to Carlsruhe for festivities to celebrate the occasion. They began with an opening of art and horticultural exhibitions, followed by his reception of a deputation of the Federal Council under the leadership of Bülow. At the weekend there was a state banquet at which several speeches were made. In proposing the health of the Emperor, the Grand Duke spoke of the ties of political and family relationship which had united him with the previous two Emperors. Emperor William then rose to his feet and spoke of the Grand Duke as not only having been a faithful ally of Emperor William I and a champion of his ideas, but also as a pattern to the younger generation, to which he himself belonged.

> For me it can only be the highest honour, as it awakens in me the most profound gratitude, to hear from the lips of the representative of the generation of my grandfather that your Royal Highness agrees with the principles on which I endeavour to govern. For it shows that these principles keep on the lines laid down for us by my grandfather of immortal memory.[14]

That evening the whole of Carlsruhe was illuminated. The students from the universities of Heidelberg and Freiburg and the technical college staged a torchlight procession, and loudly cheered the Grand Duke and Emperor when they appeared on the balcony of the castle.

During the first decade of the twentieth century, the Grand Duke and Duchess were regularly concerned by the prospect of war breaking out. In the spring of 1905

Emperor William was persuaded by Bülow and Baron von Holstein, his Foreign Minister, to visit Morocco. The Chancellor and his advisers thought it would be as well for Germany to administer a reminder to France and Britain that they could not act unilaterally in European matters where German interests were involved. On 31 March he went to Tangier, and in a speech proclaimed to a handful of German officials and merchants that Germany would support the Sultan of Morocco's efforts to keep the country open for peaceful competition in trade among all nations. His own presence there was a pledge of Germany's growing interests. He had underestimated how sensitive the British were to anything that might be seen as intriguing by Germany for a naval station situated so close to vital trade routes. Throughout most of Europe it was accepted that the north African country was about to become a French protectorate, and Britain saw this attempt to undermine French standing as an insult to both France and Britain.

To resolve the situation, Germany demanded an international conference on the future of Morocco, and France agreed to submit the matter to such a proceeding. It was a shortlived triumph for the Emperor, and in retrospect it was seen that he had helped to foster a climate of uncertainty in which the threat of European war could not be far away.

By the end of 1905 the Emperor seemed to be dreading the possibility of eventual war, which he was anxious to avoid at least until Germany had concluded a formal alliance with Turkey. They could not unleash a conflict against France and England on their own, and the coming year would be particularly unfavourable for conflict to break out. The German military chiefs had just started a major programme of artillery renewal, expected to take at least a year. Yet the greatest obstacle to war, Bülow thought, was that his sovereign was obsessed with the 'socialist menace at home', which would prevent them from taking a single man out of the country.

In January 1906 the conference requested by Germany to settle the matter arising from Morocco was convened at Algeciras in Spain. The German delegates were supported only by Austria, and they had hoped to drive Britain and France apart, but the net result was to isolate Germany. On its conclusion in April, the conference authorised France and Spain to police the country for the Sultan under a Swiss inspector general. Germany could take comfort in the knowledge that a principle had been established whereby the country was under international, not French control. However, the Entente Cordiale had been strengthened, not weakened, as a result of the Emperor's folly the previous year, and after the loss of prestige following defeat in the Russo-Japanese war, Russia could see the advantage of an understanding, leading to an alliance, with Britain. Italy had been bound to Germany in the Triple Alliance since 1882, but King Victor Emmanuel III and his government had been repelled by Emperor William's attitude and his ministers' clumsy efforts to drive a wedge between them and France. They had done nothing at the conference to support Berlin, thus implying that they no longer regarded Germany as a valuable ally.

The Grand Duke had been particularly alarmed by the prospect of European hostilities. Appreciating that the incident had been harmful to Germany's prestige throughout the continent, he put his reasons forward in a letter to his nephew on the subject:

> Surely it must be self-evident how harmful a war with France would be for us and how unpopular in Germany. Such a war could only be desired by those who wish to impede our exports and so

ruin our highly developed industry, since that would be the result of any war, even if we were the victors on land. We should lose all our allies and could only recover them with difficulty. Thank God, Your Majesty's government is peaceful. A conciliatory policy in the Moroccan question would be received with acclamation by the whole country and would mean renewed industrial prosperity. Once France knows that her Eastern frontier is secure and that Germany sincerely wishes peace, a policy of accommodation at Algeciras will be of the greatest benefit to ourselves in spite of Alsace-Lorraine.[15]

The conference marked the first time since the end of the Franco-Prussian war that the major European powers had been shown how a territorial dispute could result in war. From this date could be marked the beginning of a crisis of confidence in the Emperor's leadership of Germany, a sense of growing fatalism and, worst of all, a resigned belief in the inevitability of conflict that would culminate in the events of the summer of 1914.

On 20 September 1906 celebrations were staged for the Grand Duke's jubilee and golden wedding anniversary. Congratulations came from all corners of Europe, and King Edward VII sent the Duke of Connaught to come and invest him in person with the Order of the Garter.

A remarkably generous if slightly barbed tribute came from the French newspaper *Le Temps*, commenting that he had spent most of his fifty years in struggling against the Catholic opposition, but 'the age of the Grand Duke, the perfect dignity of his life, his tact, and his real moderation have placed him outside and above those politico-religious conflicts.' He owed his title to the will of Napoleon, who had originally transformed the margraviate of Baden and raised it to a Grand Duchy about a hundred years earlier, had done France

> all the harm he could. But French opinion itself renders justice to the probity of his character and to the ardour of his patriotism, and nobody will feel surprise at the homage with which Germany feels bound to surround his old age.[16]

A banquet was held at the palace at Carlsruhe at which the Emperor raised a toast to his uncle and aunt. He then made a graceful speech in which he referred to the great days of the German Fatherland, and expressed the hope that so long as a German heart beat in a German bosom nobody should forget who the first man was that raised his voice to point out the right path for the fulfilment of the desire of the German people for the reconstruction of a German Empire, and who had first greeted the newly-risen Emperor for whom the people had so long yearned.

Throughout his life the Grand Duke had enjoyed the best of health. A few days after his eighty-first birthday in September 1907, he became ill. It was thought that he had contracted an internal chill while attending the consecration of a Catholic church at Litzelstatten on a particularly cold day and had a slight temperature. The Grand Duchess and the Crown Princess of Sweden came to his bedside at Mainau to nurse him, while high officers of the Court and representatives of the government assembled there, as bulletins alerted the public to his deteriorating condition. The Crown Prince of Sweden was on his way to join them, but arrived just too late as his father-in-law passed away on the morning of 28 September, and the Grand Ducal Standard was lowered to half-mast on the towers of Mainau to tell the people that their sovereign was dead.

His body lay in state in the chapel of the castle at Carlsruhe until the funeral took place on 6 October. An imposing array of German and European royalty attended the ceremonies, including the Emperor William, his brother Henry and their youngest sister Margaret, the Duke of Connaught from England, Crown Prince Gustav of Sweden, Prince Albert of Belgium, Prince Henry of the Netherlands, and Grand Duke Nicholas Michaelovich of Russia.

Their son and heir succeeded as Grand Duke, taking the style of Frederick II. His marriage was childless, and the new heir to the Grand Duchy was now his cousin, Prince Max of Baden.

II

JUST over two months after the death of the
Grand Duke, on 8 December 1907, King Oscar of
Sweden died at the age of seventy-eight after a
short illness. He was succeeded by his eldest son, who
took the title of King Gustav V, and Louise's daughter
Victoria thus came into her inheritance as Queen
Consort.

Although she still spent several months abroad
during, before and after the winter months, she still
ruled the Swedish court with a rod of iron. Having
been none too pleased when her eldest son Gustav
Adolf fell in love with and married a British princess,
Margaret of Connaught, in 1905, she resolved to have
some influence over the marriage of her second son
William to Grand Duchess Maria Pavlovna of Russia,
a granddaughter of Tsar Alexander II through his
youngest son Grand Duke Paul, in May 1908.

While she followed in the family tradition set by
her mother and grandmother before her of helping to
encourage charities, involvement in good works did
not make her any the more popular. Very strict with
regard to discipline, it was said that if members of the
palace guard ever forgot to salute her, they would
generally be placed under arrest. Swedish court life
was dominated by tremendous stiffness, upheld to the
letter by the Queen's much-favoured lady in waiting,
Helen Taube.

Like the citizens of their Scandinavian
neighbours Norway, Denmark and the Russian grand

duchy of Finland, the Swedes had no great love for the German empire. Nevertheless the passionately pro-German Queen continued to maintain a strong Teutonic influence over her easily-swayed husband. In the first year of their reign, they paid an official visit to Berlin at which they were eagerly welcomed by the German Emperor William and Empress Augusta Victoria, as well as the Dowager Grand Duchess of Baden, delighted to welcome her daughter as a Queen. Described by contemporaries as very strict and militant in personality, with the heart of a Prussian soldier, Victoria was very pleased when an honorary Prussian Colonelcy was conferred on her.

True to her Prussian origins, she was always ultra-conservative in her political views. She looked with the utmost dismay on the dissolution of the Swedish-Norwegian union in 1905 which resulted in Norway becoming an independent kingdom under Prince Charles of Denmark, a grandson of King Christian IX, as King Haakon VII. Likewise the Great Strike in Sweden of 1909, and the 1911 election victory of the radicals and the Socialists as well as the liberals were also signs of a modern world that appeared to have taken leave of its senses. When Crown Prince Gustav Adolf was appointed temporary regent during the King's brief indisposition in 1912, she wrote him several letters from Italy, warning him fervently that he should take care not to be too 'intimate' with members of the elected government, whom she regarded as dangerous revolutionaries if not potential republicans.

How the Dowager Grand Duchess of Baden viewed the events of the German empire during the last six years of an uncertain peace, one can only guess, but it is unlikely that they gave her any real pleasure, or helped to make her old age a contented one. The year 1908 proved something of an *annus horribilis* for the Emperor, with a succession of problems. A homosexual scandal in which some of his friends, notably the diplomat Philipp, Count zu Eulenburg, was compounded by the embarrassment that October of what has gone down in history as the '*Daily Telegraph* interview', an article in the British press in which he castigated almost everybody, British and Germans alike, and made some foolish criticisms and admissions. The result was to provoke major criticism from authorities and subjects in both countries, lead him to something approaching a nervous breakdown, and a threat to abdicate in favour of his eldest son Crown Prince William. Neither was he on the best of terms with his siblings. While he had previously been close to the two eldest, Charlotte, Hereditary Princess of Saxe-Meiningen, and Henry, he had antagonized them both at various times. The former and her husband Bernhard had little but contempt for the Emperor, while the latter was still supportive out of a sense of family duty but not really very close to him.

Apart from the Empress, who increasingly became his rock, his aunt Louise was probably the only member of the family in whom he still really felt free to confide. She was the sole survivor of his parents' generation, a link with happier days in the past, and over the years she had gradually become the mother figure he sometimes felt he never really had. In February 1909 he complained to her that he felt he was moving about

> in an atmosphere of dishonesty, mistrust, watchfulness and insincerity. One hides one's anxious thoughts and feelings for fear that they could be misinterpreted by people of ill will. Questioning, doubting faces everywhere, and sullen people performing their tasks half-heartedly. A very perceptible reaction against

the events of last November has begun among the people and in public opinion. One feels duped into believing one has committed an act of enormous folly or blatant injustice.[1]

It was doubtless partly her support, as well as that of the Empress, that helped him to recover something of his old self-confidence for the next few years. One year later, he was writing to her of his contempt for King George I of Greece and the latter's respect for democracy and the constitution. Such a state of affairs, he fulminated, might lead him to war with Turkey 'just for the sake of the constitutional principle that the King must in absolutely every case do what the chamber and the people demand!'[2] Although she had not been one to 'meddle' in politics, Louise had never shown any of her late sister-in-law's enthusiasm for democratic opinion and probably shared his views wholeheartedly, possibly even encouraging him in them.

On 4 May 1913 her son, Grand Duke Frederick, narrowly escaped being attacked. He had come from Carlsruhe to the races at Mannheim, and was entering his railway carriage at the station, when a man with an open knife in his hand sprang on to the step of the carriage. The Grand Duke struck him under the chin and pushed him away so that he fell backwards. After his arrest, the assailant 'made a confused statement' in which he said he was a paper-hanger and wanted to present a petition.[3] It later turned out that he had been frequently under treatment for chronic alcoholism and was drunk at the time of the incident.

In August 1914 Germany found herself at war, in alliance with Austria-Hungary, against the Entente Cordiale of Britain and France and their ally Russia.

Now an elderly lady of seventy-five, the grand matriarch of the family who increasingly resembled her mother in looks if not in personality, the Dowager Grand Duchess was too old to think of taking part in active nursing activities. Such duties had long since been passed on to the next generation. Yet she still maintained an active interest in welfare services and gave financial support to her daughter-in-law in Baden as well as to her niece in Berlin, the Empress Augusta Victoria, on whom much of the royal work in Germany now devolved.

Royal families across Europe now found themselves with brothers, sisters and cousins on opposite sides. In Roumania King Carol, a member of the Catholic branch of the Hohenzollern family, had not surprisingly always been very pro-German. However he was at odds with the Roumanian government as well as with his heir Crown Prince Ferdinand, who was married to Marie. The latter, a granddaughter of Queen Victoria of England through her second son Alfred, Duke of Edinburgh and briefly of Saxe-Coburg Gotha as well, had always been passionately pro-British. King Carol died in October 1914, a few weeks after the outbreak of hostilities. Less than two years into his reign King Ferdinand and his ministers sided with the Entente powers.

Many of his closest relatives in other countries looked on his declaration of allegiance against Germany with deep dismay, and Louise was foremost among the family in regarding his behaviour with disgust. Queen Marie of Roumania's brother-in-law Ernest. Prince of Hohenlohe-Langenburg, wrote to the Dowager Grand Duchess that he shared wholeheartedly in her feelings. 'How intensely I can identify with what you are feeling now,' he wrote. 'That a Hohenzollern is playing such a role one would never have thought possible in the old days.'[4] The 'old days' had given way to a new era which neither of them fully understood.

Throughout her life Louise had always been a staunch upholder of the honour of the Hohenzollern family, especially with regard to the divisive issue of the possible marriage between her niece Victoria and Prince Alexander of Battenberg that had once so embittered family relationships. During her father's lifetime, she had been one of the fiercest opponents of the scheme. After it had become clear that the marriage could never take place, in 1890 Victoria had married Prince Adolf of Schaumburg-Lippe, who died in 1916. Both women were now widows, although nearly thirty years apart in age, united in their loneliness.

During the war, Carlsruhe suffered severely from French bombing raids. On two occasions, in June 1915 and again twelve months later, there was considerable loss of life among the civilian population. In the earlier raid, the castle sustained some damage, and the Dowager Grand Duchess and the Queen of Sweden were fortunate to remain unhurt. In autumn the following year, shortly after the death of her husband, the Princess of Schaumburg-Lippe visited her aunt there. On arrival the first thing Victoria was shown was the way to the cellar, where she could go for shelter in the event of another raid. As she walked around the streets, she was astonished to see that the number of windows still left broken and unrepaired after the explosions easily outnumbered those which were still whole.[5]

Almost from the outbreak of war, the German politicians and military chiefs had hoped that they could win over the neutral country of Sweden to the cause of the Central Powers. The Scandinavian kingdom was strategically important as it protected the German army from the north, and as it offered full access to world markets for trade. Sweden was its saviour in continuing to supply Germany with iron ore. The relationship had traditionally been stronger between Sweden and the German empire than that of the other Scandinavian nations, especially among the Swedish upper classes. Vocal conservative and military circles in Stockholm particularly wished to join in the war on the side of Germany. Since the strike of 1900, King Oscar and Queen Sophie had both feared the radical elements on the left, and were worried that revolutionaries would take over Sweden. They gave their support to the conservative parties and did what they could to try and prevent the rise of the country's socialists in parliament.

Despite their mutual antipathy as a married couple, the Queen still brought a considerable pro-German influence to bear on her husband. After the outbreak of war she gave a personal gift to every Swedish volunteer who had enlisted in the German forces, and kept in close touch with the German Emperor, whom she still visited on a regular basis. Most importantly of all, she oversaw the foundation of the *Drottningens centralkomittée* ('The Queen's Central Committee'), which undertook the task of organising individual aid programmes and their mutual coordination, and with what was being done by the state and local authorities. She presided over the working committee, which gave economic assistance to the most needy families, provided the less well-off municipalities with kitchen equipment, thus enabling them to provide children with free meals, provided carbide lamps for poor homes and paid out sums of money to families which had suffered from the ravages of the Spanish influenza epidemic that claimed so many lives across Europe at the end of the war.

There had naturally been some disagreement within the family when Prince Crown Prince Gustav Adolf took as his wife Princess Margaret of Connaught, daughter of Queen Victoria's only surviving son Arthur, Duke of Connaught, as both were very supportive of Britain and her allies. Nevertheless they agreed to respect each others' differences of allegiance. They were united in their wish to ease the plight of those who were suffering as a result of the war, and the Queen's efforts helped to reverse her unpopularity to some extent.

All the same, the Queen resented Swedish social democratic election victories in 1917 and tried to prevent members of the party from joining the government. Such political influence as she possessed in what was becoming an increasingly democratic country, much to her dissatisfaction, was founded upon the power position of the German Emperor. To her mother she complained about her difficult position in Sweden, 'where the brutal pressure of England weighed heavily on the neutrals'.[6]

When revolution came to Kiel and then Berlin in November 1918 at the end of the First World War, with a war-weary nation bitter at four years of sacrifice and then defeat, seeking revenge on the monarchy which they held responsible, Louise was within less than a month of her eightieth birthday. Although she was no longer active in the nursing profession, she gladly played her part in being present to welcome back wounded German soldiers as they returned home from French prison camps.

With sadness she witnessed the overthrow of the German monarchies and the grand ducal houses. At the time of the cessation of hostilities, Queen Victoria of Sweden was at Carlsruhe on a visit to the family. Her nephew Emperor William had to abdicate, a decision forced on him much against his will, partly by another nephew Prince Max, who had the dubious honour of being the last imperial chancellor of Germany. He went into exile in Holland for the remaining twenty-two years of his life.

It was not long before the riots which had broken out in Berlin spread to Carlsruhe as well. On 11 November, the son of a courtier led a group of soldiers up to the front of the palace, followed by a large crowd. Several shots were fired as a warning, but nobody was injured. Nevertheless, the family felt it would be better if they moved away to safety while the situation was so volatile. Revolution had broken out in Kiel and then war-weary Berlin, and the family dreaded a possible repetition of the events in St Petersburg which had followed the end of the Russian empire the previous year. They quietly left the palace by the back for the safety of the Zwingenberg palace in the Neckar valley.

The new republican government gave them permission to stay at the Langenstein Palace, which belonged to a Swedish noble family. Orders were given that the former grand ducal family was to be protected, and that Langenstein should be granted exemption from housing the returning soldiers as the Queen of Sweden was in their company, and it was felt wise not to do anything that might offend their Scandinavian near-neighbour. When the Grand Duke abdicated later that month, the Socialists in the chamber passed a resolution expressing warm recognition and gratitude for his services as ruler.

Early the following year, the family sought approval from the government to live on the island of Mainau. Back came word that they were now private citizens and could do as they wished, on condition that they did not undertake any 'political activity' on behalf of the imperial family. Like her husband, the former

Dowager Duchess had always been popular, and she was allowed to spend her remaining years in retirement at Baden-Baden, and divided her time between the old grand duchy and Mainau. In March 1919 the government concluded financial arrangements with the Grand Duke. All his estates became state property, but he was allowed to retain three small castles and surrender all other possessions which were not his private property, and he was granted a payment of several million marks in settlement of all claims.

By now Louise's son Frederick, the former Grand Duke, was in indifferent health, and her daughter-in-law Hilda was the most visible presence. Contemporaries described her as a likeable, cheerful lady who was noted for her optimistic nature and sense of good humour. Like Louise before her, she had readily taken the lead in charitable provision and helping to found several schools in Baden which bore her name.

One younger member of the German princely families would always have good reason to revere Louise's memory. Hermine, daughter of Prince Henry XXII of Reuss, born in 1887, had been orphaned at the age of fourteen, her mother having died when she was still an infant. Louise and Frederick readily gave her a home at Carlsruhe and treated her like their own daughter. She was pleased to live just long enough to see her favourite nephew, having lost the throne at the end of the First World War and then his first wife the Empress, who had been in poor health by the end of the war and deteriorated sharply during their exile, dying in April 1921, take Hermine (by then a war widow with five young children of her own) as his second wife. Though the marriage was fiercely resented by most of the Emperor's children and did not prove the happiest of unions, she provided company and some solace for the former monarch in his last two decades of life. Having been in loco parentis to her for a while, Louise was doubtless supportive of their marriage in November 1922.

In the spring of 1923 she became ill. She had seen many changes during her long life, with the kingdom Prussia into which she was born raised to the leading state in a German empire under her father, and then becoming a republic after the defeat and abdication of her nephew. It was as well that she did not live to see the fate that was to befall the Weimar republic after a few years and the rise of Adolf Hitler.

It was at her home at Baden that she died peacefully on 24 April, aged eighty-four. With her death, *The Times* noted, 'there passes another of the links with the past age of Germany before the Empire, the age of the Emperor William I and Bismarck.'[7] No other member of the royal house could recall the events of seventy years ago or more, or the age of the revolutions of 1848. She was laid to rest at Carlsruhe beside her husband.

Frederick, the ex-Grand Duke of Baden, outlived his mother by only five years and died on 8 August 1928 at the age of seventy-one. His widow Hilda followed him to the grave on 8 February 1952, aged eighty-seven.

Queen Victoria of Sweden continued to spend several months each year far away on the island of Capri. Her visits had been interrupted by the war, and she was glad to resume her old routine. Now suffering from bronchitis, and possibly tuberculosis as well, it was simple for her to demand absence for health reasons, although boredom with Sweden, dislike of the inhospitable Scandinavian climate, and a husband with whom she was plainly incompatible undoubtedly played their part as well. Both of them had suffered sadness within the family circle for their youngest son Eric, created Duke of Västmanland, had always been sickly. He was thought to have been affected by the strong medication his mother took during pregnancy, or else sustained some injury during birth. Throughout his short life he was her 'much loved child of anxiety', suffering from epilepsy and unspecified mental issues, dying in September 1918 at the age of twenty-nine from influenza.

At length she purchased her own residence on Capri, a two-storey farmhouse that she named Casa Capriole, which she had extensively landscaped and surrounded with a park in order to afford herself maximum privacy. Almost every morning she joined her physician Axel Munthe at his home, the Villa San Michele, and they enjoyed walking around the island together. In the evenings they arranged concerts there, at which she generally played the piano. Both of them were lifelong lovers of animals and birds, and she was often to be seen walking a small dog, while he bought Castillo Barbarossa, an archaeological ruin, for preservation as a bird sanctuary.

During the little time that she still spent in Sweden, she continued to pursue her charitable initiatives. On her sixtieth birthday in August 1922, she was presented with 170,000 kroner, which she used to found a retirement home for former working women. During the next few years of her life she made occasional official visits to various parts of the country in the company of the King, up to and including what was to be a final official appearance in public on their joint visit to Finland in 1925. After a severe illness and heart trouble the following year the doctors pronounced her condition as hopeless, and provisional arrangements were made for her funeral and subsequent rites. Nevertheless she defied all expectations and made what appeared to be a satisfactory recovery.

In June 1928 she was present at the seventieth birthday celebrations held for King Gustav, among them a banquet for five hundred guests at the Stockholm Palace. But it required a considerable effort on her part, and this would be her last appearance at court. Thereafter she lived at Rome, where she had bought the Villa Swezia. After falling ill again early in the new year of 1930 and suffering several heart attacks, she lingered for a few weeks while regular bulletins were issued regarding the state of her increasingly precarious health.

She died on the evening of 4 April, at the age of sixty-seven. The King and their children had been warned that the end was approaching, and they managed to reach her side just in time.

He survived her by twenty years, dying on 29 October 1950 at the age of ninety-two, and was succeeded by their eldest son as King Gustav VI Adolf at the age of sixty-seven. He had inherited his father's longevity and lived to the age of ninety, dying on 15 September 1973. Having been long since predeceased not only by both his wives but also by his son, also Prince Gustav Adolf, who had been killed in an air crash in 1947, he was succeeded by his grandson as King Carl XVI Gustav.

Next in line to the Swedish throne is the King's eldest child, Crown Princess Victoria. Today Hohenzollern blood still flows in the Bernadotte family in a line of descent from Louise, Grand Duchess of Baden, thus ensuring that one day her great-great-granddaughter will reign in her own right as Queen Victoria of Sweden.

Princess Victoria of Baden and Crown Prince Gustav of Sweden at the time of their engagement, 1881

Crown Princess Victoria of Sweden and her sons

Prince and Princess William of Prussia and their eldest son William, 1887

The Empress Frederick, c.1896

Queen Victoria of Sweden with Prince Max von Baden (left) and her husband King Gustav V (right), c.1910

Louise and Frederick, Grand Duke and Duchess of Baden,
c.1906

The Grand Duke and Duchess of Baden, 1906

Mainau Castle

Louise, Grand Duchess of Baden, c.1910

Louise, Grand Duchess of Baden, c.1914

Louise, Grand Duchess of Baden, in her last years

Frederick II, the last Grand Duke of Baden

Queen Victoria of Sweden in her last years

THE ROYAL FAMILY OF PRUSSIA

FREDERICK WILLIAM III   m. Louise of
1770-1840   Mecklenburg-Strelitz
                           1776-1810

FREDERICK WILLIAM IV	WILLIAM I
1795-1861	1797-1888
m. Elizabeth of Bavaria	m. Augusta of Saxe-
1801-73	Weimar-Eisenach
No issue	1811-90

FREDERICK III	**Louise**
1831-88	1838-1923
m. Victoria, Princess Royal	m. Frederick
of England	1826-1907
1840-1901	
	Frederick
WILLIAM II	1857-1928
1859-1941	
	Victoria
Charlotte	1862-1930
1860-1919	
	Louis
Henry	1865-88
1862-1929	
Sigismund	
1864-6	
Victoria	
1866-1929	

[continued overleaf

Waldemar
1868-79

Sophie
1870-1932

Margaret
1872-1954

THE GRAND DUCAL FAMILY OF BADEN

LEOPOLD   m.   Sophie of Sweden
1790-1852   1801-65

Alexandrine
1820-1904
m. Ernest II, Duke of Saxe-Coburg and Gotha

Louis
b. & d.1822

LOUIS
1824-58

FREDERICK
1826-1907
m. **Louise of Prussia**

William
1829-97
m. Marie Maximilianova of Leuchtenberg

Charles
1832-1906
m. Rosalie von Beust

Marie
1834-99
m. Ernest, Prince of Leiningen

Cecilie
1839-91
m. Michael Nicolaievich, Grand Duke of Russia

THE ROYAL FAMILY OF SWEDEN

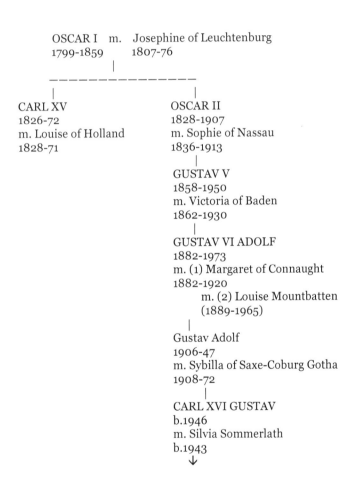

OSCAR I   m.   Josephine of Leuchtenburg
1799-1859   1807-76
|

CARL XV   OSCAR II
1826-72   1828-1907
m. Louise of Holland   m. Sophie of Nassau
1828-71   1836-1913
|

GUSTAV V
1858-1950
m. Victoria of Baden
1862-1930
|

GUSTAV VI ADOLF
1882-1973
m. (1) Margaret of Connaught
1882-1920
     m. (2) Louise Mountbatten
     (1889-1965)
|

Gustav Adolf
1906-47
m. Sybilla of Saxe-Coburg Gotha
1908-72
|

CARL XVI GUSTAV
b.1946
m. Silvia Sommerlath
b.1943
↓

CHRONOLOGY

1838
Birth of Louise Marie Elizabeth of Prussia, 3 December, at Berlin, second child and only daughter of William and Augusta, their their first child being Frederick William (born 1831), future King and Emperor

1840
Death of King Frederick William III, 7 June, and accession of Louise's uncle as Frederick William IV

1851
Louise accompanies parents and brother to London, April and May, as guests of Queen Victoria and Prince Albert, to visit Great Exhibition

1854
Louise is betrothed to Frederick, Prince Regent of Baden (born 1826), June

1856
Louise marries Frederick, 20 September, at Potsdam; Frederick takes title of Grand Duke of Baden

1857
Birth of Frederick, 9 July

1858

Death of Louis II, mentally incapacitated Grand Duke of Baden, 23 January

1861

Death of Frederick William IV, King of Prussia, 2 January, and accession of Louise's father William, Prince Regent, as William I

1862

Birth of Victoria, 7 August; appointment of Bismarck as Minister-President of Prussia, later German Chancellor, September

1865

Birth of Louis, 12 June

1866

Baden, an ally of Austria, defeated in Austro-Prussian war, July-August

1871

German victory in Franco-Prussian war leads to proclamation of German Empire at Versailles, 18 January, with King William assuming title of German Emperor

1878

Louise and Emperor William are unhurt after Max Hödel attempts to assassinate the latter in Berlin, 11 May

1881

Victoria marries Crown Prince Gustav of Sweden and Norway, 20 September

1885
Frederick marries Princess Hilda of Nassau, 20 September

1888
Deaths of Louis, 23 February, Emperor William I, 9 March, and Emperor Frederick III, 15 June; accession of Emperor William II

1890
Death of Empress Augusta, 7 January; resignation of Bismarck as Chancellor, March

1902
Grand Duke of Baden's fiftieth anniversary of accession commemorated, April

1906
Grand Duke and Duchess of Baden's jubilee and golden wedding anniversary commemorated, 20 September

1907
Death of Frederick I, Grand Duke of Baden, 28 September, and accession of son as Frederick II; death of Oscar II, King of Sweden, and accession of Louise's daughter Victoria's husband as Gustav V, 8 December

1914
Outbreak of First World War, 4 August

1918
Abdication of Emperor William II and declaration of German republic at end of First World War, November

1919
Former grand ducal family of Baden given permission by government to reside in Mainau

1923
Death of Louise, Grand Duchess of Baden, 24 April

1928
Death of Frederick II, former Grand Duke of Baden, 9 August

1930
Death of Victoria, Queen of Sweden, 4 April

REFERENCE NOTES

1. DAUGHTER OF THE EMPEROR (pp.7-46)

I

1 Tschudi, 52
2 *Ibid*, 91-2
3 Bennett, 65
4 Roberts, 17
5 Pakula, 51, Queen Victoria to King Leopold, 27.5.1851
6 *Alice*, 9-10
7 *Further Letters*, 47-8, Queen Victoria to Princess Augusta, 30.5.1854
8 Albert, *Letters of the Prince Consort*, 215, Prince Albert to Prince William, 6.6.1854
9 *The Times*, 23 September 1856
10 Albert, *Letters of the Prince Consort*, 264, Prince Albert to Princess Augusta, 24.9.1856
11 Anon., *Recollections of three Kaisers*, 35
12 Victoria, Queen, *Dearest Child*, 212, Queen Victoria to Princess Frederick William, 11.10.1859
13 Roberts, 47
14 Röhl, *Young Wilhelm: The Kaiser's early life*, 64, Princess Frederick William to Queen Victoria, 24.3.1859
15 *Ibid*, 98, Crown Princess Frederick William to Queen Victoria, 23.1.1861
16 Victoria, Queen, *Dearest Child*, 95, Princess Frederick William to Queen Victoria, 24.4.1858
17 *Ibid*, 212, Princess Frederick William to Queen Victoria, 24.4.1858

18 *Ibid*, 289, Princess Frederick William to Queen Victoria, 7.12.1860

19 *Ibid*, 303, Queen Victoria to Crown Princess Frederick William, 16.1.1861

20 *Ibid*, 355, Queen Victoria to Crown Princess Frederick William, 5.10.1861

21 Victoria, Queen, *Dearest Mama*, 41, Crown Princess Frederick William to Queen Victoria, 13.1.1862

22 *Alice*, 18-19

23 Victoria, Queen, *Dearest Mama*, 107, Crown Princess Frederick William to Queen Victoria, 10.9.1862

24 Victoria, Queen, *Your Dear Letter*, 123-4, Crown Princess Frederick William to Queen Victoria, 15.2.1867

25 Frederick, Emperor, *Diaries*, 48, 3.7.1866

26 *The Times*, 30.9.1907

27 Röhl, *Young Wilhelm: The Kaiser's early life,* 146, Crown Princess Frederick William to Crown Prince, 9.6.1867

28 Müller, 25

29 *The Times*, 30.9.1907

30 Taylor, 132

31 Frederick, *War Diary*, 272-3, 18.1.1871

II

1 *The Tablet*, 28.2.1874

2 *The Times*, 25.4.1923

3 Victoria, Queen, *Darling Child*, 82, Crown Princess Frederick William to Queen Victoria, 24.3.1873

4 William II, Ex-Emperor, *My Early Life*, 87

5 Röhl, *Young Wilhelm: The Kaiser's early life*, 291, Crown Princess Frederick William to Crown Prince, 28.9.1877

6 *Ibid*, 290, William to Louise, 31.5.1878

7 *Ibid,* 362, Grand Duchess of Baden to Hermann zu Hohenlohe-Langenburg, 25-6.2.1881

8 *The Times,* 21.9.1981

9 Herbert, 191

10 Radziwill, 153

11 Victoria, Queen, *Beloved Mama*, 134, Crown Princess Frederick William to Queen Victoria, 6.3.1883

12 *Ibid*, 135, Queen Victoria to Crown Princess Frederick William, 14.3.1883

13 Victoria, Queen, *Beloved and Darling Child*, 41, Crown Princess Frederick William to Queen Victoria, 5.10.1886

14 Pakula, 438, Crown Princess Frederick William to Queen Victoria, 22.5.1887

15 *The Times*, 24.2.1888

16 Wiegler, 441

2. AUNT TO THE EMPEROR (pp.63-92)

I

1 Pakula, 511, Empress Frederick to Queen Victoria, 20.10.1888

2 Victoria, *Letters of the Empress Frederick*, 326, Empress Frederick to Queen Victoria, 5.7.1888

3 Tschudi, 235

4 Pakula, 524, Empress Frederick to Queen Victoria, 23.1.1890

5 Ludwig, 70

6 *The Times*, 30.9.1907

7 Victoria, *Empress Frederick writes to Sophie*, 111

8 Röhl, *Wilhelm II: The Kaiser's personal monarchy*, pp. 513-4

9 Victoria, *Empress Frederick writes to Sophie*, 205-6

10 Pakula, 587, Empress Frederick to Queen Victoria, 21.4.1900

11 Bülow, *My Memoirs, 1897-1903*, 481

12 *Ibid*, 428

13 Röhl, *Wilhelm II: Into the abyss of war and exile,* 4, Grand Duchess of Baden to Emperor William, 26.1.1901

14 *The Times*, 28.4.1902
14 Bülow, *My Memoirs*, 1903-1909, 201
15 *The Times*, 22.9.1906

II

1 Röhl, *Wilhelm II: Into the abyss of war and exile,* 739, Emperor William to Grand Duchess of Baden, 5.2.1909
2 *Ibid*, 755, Emperor William to Grand Duchess of Baden, 1.2.1910
3 *The Times*, 5.5.1913
4 Urbach, 97, Prince Ernest of Hohenlohe-Langenburg to Grand Duchess of Baden, 18.9.1916
5 Victoria of Prussia, *My Memoirs*, 186
6 Urbach, 103
7 *The Times*, 25.4.1923

BIBLIOGRAPHY

Books

Albert, Prince Consort, *Letters of the Prince Consort, 1831-1861,* ed. Kurt Jagow (London: John Murray, 1938)

Alice, Grand Duchess of Hesse, Princess of Great Britain and Ireland, Biographical Sketch and Letters (London: John Murray, 1884)

Anon., *Recollections of three Kaisers* (London: Herbert Jenkins, 1929)

Austin, Paul Britten, tr., *The Bernadottes: Their political and cultural achievements* (Läcko: Stiftelsen Läckö Institutet, 1991)

Bennett, Daphne, *Vicky, Princess Royal of England and German Empress* (London: Collins Harvill, 1971)

Bülow, Prince Bernhard von, *My Memoirs, 1897-1903* (London: Putnam, 1931)

-- *My Memoirs,* 1903-1909 (London: Putnam, 1931)

Corti, Egon Caesar Conte, *The English Empress: A study in the relations between Queen Victoria and her eldest daughter, Empress Frederick of Germany* (London: Cassell, 1957)

Frederick, Emperor, *Diaries of the Emperor Frederick during the Campaigns of 1866 and 1870-71, as well as his Journeys to the east and to Spain,* ed. Margarethe von Poschinger (London: Chapman & Hall, 1902)

-- *The war diary of the Emperor Frederick III*, ed. A.R. Allinson (London: Stanley Paul, 1927)

Herbert, Basil, *King Gustave of Sweden* (London: Stanley Paul, 1938)

Ludwig, Emil, *Kaiser Wilhelm II* (London: Putnam, 1926)

MacDonogh, Giles, *The last Kaiser: William the impetuous* (London: Weidenfeld & Nicolson, 2000)

Müller, Frank Lorenz, *Our Fritz: Emperor Frederick III and the political culture of imperial Germany* (Harvard University Press, 2011)

Noel, Gerard, *Princess Alice: Queen Victoria's Forgotten Daughter* (London: Constable, 1974)

Pakula, Hanah, *An uncommon woman: The Empress Frederick* (London: Weidenfeld & Nicolson, 1996)

Radziwill, Catherine, *The Empress Frederick* (London: Cassell, 1934)

Roberts, Dorothea, *Two royal lives: Gleanings from Berlin and from the lives of Their Imperial Highnesses The Crown Prince and Princess of Germany* (London: T. Fisher Unwin, 1888)

Röhl, John C.G., *Young Wilhelm: The Kaiser's early life, 1859-1888* (Cambridge: Cambridge University Press, 1998)

-- *Wilhelm II: The Kaiser's personal monarchy, 1888-1900* (Cambridge: Cambridge University Press, 2004)

-- *Wilhelm II: Into the abyss of war and exile, 1900-1941* (Cambridge: Cambridge University Press, 2014)

Taylor, A.J.P., *Bismarck: The man and the statesman* (London: Hamish Hamilton, 1955)

Tschudi, Clara, *Augusta, Empress of Germany* (London: Swan Sonnenschein, 1900)

Urbach, Karina, *Go-betweens for Hitler* (Oxford: Oxford University Press, 2015)

Van der Kiste, John, *The first German Empress: Augusta, Consort of Emperor William I* (South Brent: A&F/CreateSpace, 2016)
-- *Northern Crowns: The Kings of Modern Scandinavia* (Stroud: Sutton, 1996)
Victoria, Queen, *Dearest Child: Letters between Queen Victoria and the Princess Royal*, ed. Roger Fulford (London: Evans Bros, 1964)
-- *Dearest Mama: Private Correspondence of Queen Victoria and the Crown Princess of Prussia, 1861-1864;* ed. Roger Fulford (London: Evans Bros, 1968)
-- *Your Dear Letter: Private Correspondence of Queen Victoria and the Crown Princess of Prussia, 1865-1871;* ed. Roger Fulford (London: Evans Bros, 1971)
-- *Beloved Mama: Private Correspondence of Queen Victoria and the German Crown Princess, 1878-1885;* ed. Roger Fulford (London: Evans Bros, 1981)
-- *Beloved and darling child: Last letters between Queen Victoria and her eldest daughter, 1886-1901;* ed. Agatha Ramm (Stroud: Sutton, 1990)
-- *Further letters of Queen Victoria: From the Archives of the House of Brandenburg-Prussia,* ed. Hector Bolitho (London: Thornton Butterworth, 1938)
Victoria, Consort of Frederick III, German Emperor, *The Empress Frederick writes to Sophie, her daughter, Crown Princess and later Queen of the Hellenes,* ed. Arthur Gould Lee (London: Faber, 1955)
-- *Letters of the Empress Frederick,* ed. Sir Frederick Ponsonby (London: Macmillan, 1928)
Victoria of Prussia, Princess, *My memoirs* (London: Eveleigh, Nash & Grayson, 1929)

Wiegler, Paul, *William the First, His life and times* (London: Allen & Unwin, 1929)

William II, Ex-Emperor, *My early life* (London: Methuen, 1926)

Journals

Royalty Digest
The Tablet
The Times

INDEX

Adolf, Grand Duke of Luxembourg (1817-1905) 40

Albert I, King of the Belgians (1875-1934) 79

Albert, Prince Consort of Great Britain (1819-61) invites Prussian royal family to Great Exhibition 11; death 23

Alexander II, Tsar of Russia (1818-81) 80

Alexander III, Tsar of Russia (1845-94), 41

Alexander of Battenberg, Prince of Bulgaria (1857-93) 41, 43-4

Alexandra, Queen of Great Britain (1844-1925) 22-3

Alexandrine, Duchess of Saxe-Coburg-Gotha (1820-1904) 14

Alfred, Duke of Edinburgh and Saxe-Coburg Gotha (1844-1900) 84

Alice, Grand Duchess of Hesse and the Rhine (1843-78) 12, 40; proposed as wife for William of Baden, and marriage to Louis of Hesse 21; and death of Prince Consort 23; and friendship with Louise 23; death 40

Arthur, Duke of Connaught and Strathearn (1850-1942) 79, 87

Augusta, German Empress (1811-90) 9, 33, 63; character and marriage, 7, 10; invited to England 11-2; coldness to family 21; becomes Queen 22; and charity work 26; ill-health 37, 42; improved relations with Louise 40, 64; at William I's deathbed 45; last illness and death 65-6

Augusta Victoria, German Empress (1858-1921) 35, 43, 67, 81, 82

Barton, Clara (1821-1912) 27

Beatrice, Princess (1857-1944) 42

Bernhard, Duke of Saxe-Meiningen (1851-1928) 66

Bismarck, Otto von (1815-98), 24, 28-33, 90; resignation 67

Blücher, Madeleine, Countess (1810-79) 18

Bray, Otto (1807-99) 27
Bülow, Bernhard von (1849-1929) 72, 74, 75

Caprivi, Leo von (1831-99) 70, 71
Carl XVI Gustav, King of Sweden (b.1946) 92
Carl, Duke of Västergötland (1861-1951) 40
Carol I, King of Roumania (1839-1914) 84
Cecilie of Baden, Princess (1839-91) 14
Charles of Baden, Prince (1832-1906) 14
Charlotte, Duchess of Saxe-Meiningen (1860-1919) 66, 82
Christian IX, King of Denmark (1818-1906) 22, 81
Constantine I, King of Greece (1868-1923) 68

Edward VII, King of Great Britain (1841-1910) 22
Elizabeth of Hesse and the Rhine, Princess, later Grand
    Duchess Serge of Russia (1864-1918) 40-1
Elizabeth, Queen of Prussia (1801-73) 9, 16
Eric, Duke of Västmanland (1889-1918) 37, 91
Ernest, Duke of Saxe-Coburg Gotha (1818-93) 14
Ernest, Prince of Hohenlohe-Langenburg (1863-1950) 84
Eugene, Duke of Närke (1865-1947) 40
Eulenburg, Philipp, Count (1847-1921) 82

Fane, John, Lord Burghersh and 11th Earl of Westmoreland
    (1784-1859) and Jane (d.1921) 12
Ferdinand, King of Roumania (1865-1927) 84
Frederick I, Grand Duke of Baden (1826-1907) 20, 41; early
    life, engagement and marriage 13-7; and friendship with
    Alice 23; and Austro-Prussian war 25; and William II, as
    Prince and Emperor 25-6, 70-1; and proclamation of
    German Empire 27-8; and government of Baden during
    imperial era 29; and Roman Catholics 30; and Bismarck
    34; and silver wedding anniversary 36; and death of
    Frederick III 63; and relations with Empress Frederick
    64; and Bismarck's resignation 67; and fiftieth
    anniversary of accession 73-4; and Tangier crisis 75-7;
    and jubilee and golden wedding 77-8; last illness, death
    and funeral 78-9
Frederick II, Grand Duke of Baden (1857-1928) 18, 35, 83,
    89; engagement and marriage 40-2; succeeds as Grand
    Duke 79; death 90

Frederick III, German Emperor (1831-88) 17, 26, 33; birth 7; invited to England for Great Exhibition 11-2; engagement and marriage 19; and Austro-Prussian war 25; and proclamation of German Empire 27-8; ill-health 42-5; reign and death 63

Frederick William III (1770-1840) 7, 8

Frederick William IV, King of Prussia (1795-1861) accession 8; death 21

George I, King of Greece (1845-1913) 83

Gustav IV Adolf, King of Sweden (1778-1837) 13

Gustav V, King of Sweden (1858-1950) 91; engagement and marriage 35-7; accession 80; death 92

Gustav VI Adolf, King of Sweden (1882-1973) 37, 80, 81, 92

Haakon VII, King of Norway (1872-1957) 81

Henry of the Netherlands, Prince (1876-1934) 79

Henry of Prussia, Prince (1862-1929) 68, 79, 82

Henry XXII, Prince of Reuss (1846-1902) 89

Henry, Prince, 131, 133, 142

Hermine, Princess of Schönaich-Carolath (1887-1947) 89

Hilda, Grand Duchess of Baden (1864-1952) 42, 89, 90

Hinzpeter, Georg (1826-1907) 26

Hitler, Adolf (1889-1945) 90

Hödel, Max (d.1878) 34

Hohenlohe-Schillingsfürst, Chlodwig von (1819-1901) 25, 27, 71

Holstein, Friedrich von (1837-1909) 75

Humboldt, Alexander von (1769-1859) 19

Irene of Hesse and the Rhine, Princess, later Princess Henry of Prussia (1866-1953) 68

Leopold I, King of the Belgians (1790-1865) 11

Leopold, Duke of Albany and Clarence (1853-84) 11

Leopold, Grand Duke of Baden (1790-1852) 13

Louis XIV, King of France (1638-1715) 10

Louis, Grand Duke of Baden (1824-58) 13-4

Louis, Grand Duke of Hesse and the Rhine (1837-92) 21, 23

Louise of Prussia, Princess, later Grand Duchess of Baden (1838-1923) birth 8; childhood 9; invited to England for

123

Great Exhibition 11-2; and friendship with Alice 12, 21, 23, 40; betrothal and marriage 13-7; and birth of Frederick 18; relationship with Crown Princess Frederick William 20, 26, 64; and Queen Augusta's coldness towards family 21; suspected of circulating rumours about Princess Christian 22-3; and births of Victoria and Louis 24; and William II as Prince and Emperor 25-6, 34, 64, 73; and charity work 26-7; and Roman Catholics 30-3; and parents' social life 34; and silver wedding anniversary, and marriage of Victoria 36; improving relations with Empress Augusta 40; and marriage of Frederick 41; and Battenberg marriage issue 41, 43-4; and William I's death 45-6; and death of Frederick III 63; and Empress Augusta's death 65-6; presented with Order of Victoria & Albert 66; and Bismarck's resignation 68; and Unter den Linden 68-9; at memorial service for Empress Frederick 73; and Grand Duke Frederick's last illness and death 78; William II confides in 82-3; and outbreak of First World War 84; invites Princess Adolf of Schaumburg-Lippe to stay 85; last years and death 87-90

Louise, Queen of Denmark, formerly Princess Christian (1817-98) 22

Louise, Queen of Prussia (1776-1810) 8

Louis of Baden, Prince (1865-88), 128

Mackenzie, Dr Morell (1837-92) 44

Marie of Baden, Princess (1834-99) 14

Marie, Queen of Roumania (1875-1938) 84

Margaret, Crown Princess of Sweden (1882-1920) 80, 87

Margaret of Prussia, Princess, later Landgravine of Hesse-Cassel (1872-1954) 79

Maximilian of Baden, Prince (1867-1929) 79

Munck, Ebba, later Ebba Bernadotte (1858-1946) 39

Munthe, Axel (1857-1949) 91

Napoleon III, Emperor of the French (1808-73) 27

Nicholas Michaelovich, Grand Duke of Russia (1859-1919) 79

Nightingale, Florence (1820-1910), 26

Oscar II, King of Norway and Sweden (1829-1907), 36, 80, 86

Oscar, Count of Wisborg (1859-1953) 39

Paul Alexandrovich, Grand Duke of Russia (1860-1919) 80

Radziwill, Elise (1803-34) 7, 46

Serge Alexandrovich, Grand Duke of Russia (1857-1905) 41
Sophie, Queen of Norway and Sweden (1836-1913) 36, 86
Sophie, Queen of Greece (1870-1932) 68, 71
Sophie, Grand Duchess of Baden (1801-65) 13
Stöcker, Adolf (1835-1909) 43
Strauss, David (1808-74) 40

Taube, Helen 80

Victor Emmanuel III, King of Italy (1869-1947) 76
Victoria, Queen of Great Britain (1819-1901) 13, 14, 18, 20, 23, 24, 42, 43, 66, 71, 84, 87; invites Prussian royal family to Great Exhibition 11; and chances of Elizabeth of Hesse's marriage to Frederick of Baden 40-1; death 72-3
Victoria, Queen of Sweden (1862-1930) 88; birth 24; engagement, wedding and character 33-9, 80; and ill-health 37-8; and father's death 78; and Gustav V's accession to throne 80; German influence on Gustav V, and political views 81, 87; last years and death 90-2
Victoria, Crown Princess of Sweden (b.1980) 92
Victoria of Hesse and the Rhine, Princess (1863-1950) 42
Victoria of Prussia, Princess (1866-1929) 78, 105, 121, 125, 127, 142
Victoria Louise, Duchess of Brunswick (1892-1980) 35
Victoria, Princess of Prussia (1866-1929) 41, 43-4, 85
Victoria, Princess Royal of Great Britain, later German Empress Victoria, later Empress Frederick (1840-1901) 17, 22, 24, 33, 71; at Great Exhibition 11; and relationship with Louise 20, 42, 68, 69; and Queen Augusta's coldness 21; and antipathy between King William and Queen Augusta 22; and chances of Elizabeth of Hesse's marriage to Frederick of Baden 40-1; and Frederick III's

illness and death 43-5, 63; widowhood 64; death 73

Waldersee, Alfred von (1834-1904) 69, 70
William I, German Emperor (1797-1888) 26, 27, 30, 33, 37, 68, 90; character and marriage 7; fondness for Louise 10; invited to England 11; becomes King 22; and proclamation of German Empire 27-8; ill-health and death 42-5
William II, German Emperor (1859-1941) 20, 41, 43, 46, 71, 78, 79, 81; and relations with Louise and Frederick 34, 64; as a student 35; at Queen Victoria's deathbed 71-2; at Grand Duke of Baden's fiftieth anniversary celebrations 74; and Tangier crisis 75-6; and problems of 1908 82; confides increasingly in Louise 82-3; abdication and second marriage 89
William, Duke of Södermanland (1884-1965) 37, 80
William of Baden, Prince (1829-97) 13, 21
Winterhalter, Franz Xaver (1805-73) 17

Also by John Van der Kiste

Royal and historical biography

Frederick III (1981)
Queen Victoria's Family: A Select Bibliography
  (1982)
Dearest Affie [with Bee Jordaan] (1984)
  - revised edition, *Alfred* (2014)
Queen Victoria's Children (1986)
Windsor and Habsburg (1987)
Edward VII's Children (1989)
Princess Victoria Melita (1991)
George V's Children (1991)
George III's Children (1992)
Crowns in a Changing World (1993)
Kings of the Hellenes (1994)
Childhood at Court 1819-1914 (1995)
Northern Crowns (1996)
King George II and Queen Caroline (1997)
The Romanovs 1818-1959 (1998)
Kaiser Wilhelm II (1999)
The Georgian Princesses (2000)
Dearest Vicky, Darling Fritz (2001)
Royal Visits to Devon & Cornwall (2002)
Once a Grand Duchess [with Coryne Hall] (2002)
William and Mary (2003)
Emperor Francis Joseph (2005)
Sons, Servants & Statesmen (2006)
A Divided Kingdom (2007)
William John Wills (2011)
The Prussian Princesses (2014)
The Big Royal Quiz Book (2014)

Prince Henry of Prussia (2015)
The last German Empress (2015)
Princess Helena (2015)
Charlotte and Feodora (2015)
Dictionary of Royal Biographers (2015)
The first German Empress (2016)
Queen Victoria and the European Empires (2016)
Of Royalty and Drink (2017)
The end of the German Monarchy (2017)

Local history and true crime

Devon Murders (2006)
Devonshire's Own (2007)
Cornish Murders [with Nicola Sly] (2007)
A Grim Almanac of Devon (2008)
Somerset Murders [with Nicola Sly] (2008)
Cornwall's Own (2008)
Plymouth, History and Guide (2009)
A Grim Almanac of Cornwall (2009)
West Country Murders [with Nicola Sly] (2009)
Jonathan Wild (2009)
Durham Murders & Misdemeanours (2009)
Surrey Murders (2009)
Berkshire Murders (2010)
More Cornish Murders [with Nicola Sly] (2010)
Ivybridge & South Brent Through Time [with Kim
    Van der Kiste] (2010)
Dartmoor from old photographs (2010)
A Grim Almanac of Hampshire (2011)
The Little Book of Devon (2011)
More Devon Murders (2011)
More Somerset Murders [with Nicola Sly] (2011)
The Plymouth Book of Days (2011)
The Little Book of Cornwall (2013)
Plymouth, a City at War 1914-45 (2014)

Music

Roxeventies (1982)
Singles File (1987)
Beyond the Summertime [with Derek Wadeson] (1990)
Gilbert & Sullivan's Christmas (2000)
Roy Wood (2014)
Jeff Lynne (2015)
The Big Music Quiz Book (2015)
Pop Pickers and Music Vendors (2016)
A Beatles Miscellany (2016)
We Can Swing Together (2017)
Electric Light Orchestra: Song by Song (2017)

Fiction

The Man on the Moor (2004)
Olga and David (2014)
Elmore Sounds (2015)
Always There (2015)

Plays and poems

The Man on the Moor (2015)
A Mere Passing Shadow (2015)
Dartmoor and other places (2015)

For availability of the above titles, please refer to Amazon.co.uk/Amazon.com

Made in the USA
Lexington, KY
14 March 2019